How to Stop Living and Start Worrying

How to Stop Living and Start Worrying

Conversations with Carl Cederström

Simon Critchley

polity

Copyright © Simon Critchley & Carl Cederström 2010

The right of Simon Critchley & Carl Cederström to be identified as Authors of
this Work has been asserted in accordance with the UK Copyright, Designs and
Patents Act 1988.

First published in 2010 by Polity Press

Polity Press
65 Bridge Street
Cambridge CB2 1UR, UK

Polity Press
350 Main Street
Malden, MA 02148, USA

ISBN-13: 978-0-7456-5038-8
ISBN-13: 978-0-7456-5039-5 (pb)

A catalogue record for this book is available from the British Library.

Typeset in 12 on 14 pt Bembo by Servis Filmsetting Ltd, Stockport, Cheshire.
Printed and bound in Great Britain by the MPG Books Group

The publisher has used its best endeavours to ensure that the URLs for external
websites referred to in this book are correct and active at the time of going to
press. However, the publisher has no responsibility for the websites and can
make no guarantee that a site will remain live or that the content is or will
remain appropriate.

Every effort has been made to trace all copyright holders, but if any have been
inadvertently overlooked the publisher will be pleased to include any necessary
credits in any subsequent reprint or edition.

For further information on Polity, visit our website: www.politybooks.com

Contents

Introduction

The conversations offered here provide an introduction and overview to the thought of Simon Critchley, one of the most influential, provocative, engaging, creative and witty philosophers of our time. In addition to discussions of the nature and tasks of philosophy, Critchley presents the reader with haunting meditations on life, death, love, humour and authenticity. All these miscellaneous subjects are treated in a reckless spirit of candour and shot through with a dark and uncompromising humour. They offer a relentlessly critical diagnosis of our time, but also a uniquely fun and easy entry into philosophy, even for those who otherwise find philosophy an arcane practice.

Simon Critchley is presently Chair and Professor of Philosophy at the New School for Social Research in New York. But his role as philosopher goes far beyond the boundaries of the university. He frequently writes for the *New York Times* and the *Guardian*, and his strenuous engagement with anarchism, the politics of resistance, social movements and experimental art practice has turned him into a spokesman for the Seattle generation, alongside Alain Badiou, Michael Hardt, Antonio Negri and Slavoj Žižek. The regrettable side-effect of this engagement, Critchley explains, is that that 'one ineluctably becomes a brand'. But Critchley seems resigned to this fate. Philosophy is not, in his words, 'a solely academic or professional activity', but an activity that involves 'exposure and risk'.

To summarize a philosopher, such as Critchley, whose

work constantly moves in various and unexpected directions, is a fraught endeavour. At best, it would involve an open invitation. At worst, it would turn a thinker into a set of stereotypes and slogans: a commodity. As will become clear from these conversations, Critchley is neither a commodity nor a brand. His work cannot be reduced to one single line of thought. As he explains: 'I devoutly hope that everything I do and say doesn't add up.'

With that caveat in mind, it can be said that Critchley's work falls squarely into the Continental tradition in philosophy. Combining close readings of Rousseau, Heidegger, Derrida, Levinas and Blanchot with accessible accounts of humour and contemporary forms of political resistance, he offers a fascinating and lively account of philosophy and the history of philosophy. Relentlessly, he has moved from subject to subject, including the intimate and complex relationship between philosophy and poetry, the problem of nihilism and humour, the relation between ethics and politics, and psychoanalysis. And what defines his approach, whether the theme is death or laughter, is that it fearlessly follows a train of thought even when it leads into morally unsafe territories. He explains: 'I sometimes follow a line simply because it interests me', and adds: 'There's no morality in writing.'

Today, philosophy is often erroneously regarded as a solipsistic activity produced by a haughty, self-professed intelligentsia that remains out of touch with the culture at large. (And there are, undeniably, circles working hard to verify that prejudice by dispassionately, and at great length, discussing things with no cultural relevance.) However, what you find in the work of Critchley is the very opposite of this tendency. Following Hegel's definition of philosophy as 'its own time comprehended in thought', he writes with a constant eye on the present, whether the subject is social movements, popular culture, or Barack Obama.

What makes these social and political analyses especially

engaging is that Critchley's personal views come to the fore. He openly applauds the subversive potential of groups like Ya Basta and the Invisible Committee, he celebrates the Marx Brothers and he looks upon the self-help movement with healthy contempt. But however ruthless he might be towards others, he always saves the most scathing mockery for himself.

This self-critical wit comes forth in many forms. We find it on a personal level, when Critchley describes how he is racked with self-doubt in his professional role as a philosopher and teacher. But more importantly, we find it in his theoretical writing, especially on humour, where he ardently defends a divided subject that is helplessly inauthentic. From psychoanalysis, Critchley takes the idea of the split subject – or what he calls the 'dividual' – which is a subject that lacks the ability to coincide with itself. This same structure or theme is also at the heart of Critchley's reading of the work of Samuel Beckett. For Critchley, Beckettian subjects are inhabitants of a sinful world in which they can neither live nor die. And yet, they strenuously move on with the courage of self-impotence.

One way to understand the concept of the dividual is in relation to today's pervasive self-help culture. Against self-help manuals, like the 1940s classic, *How to Stop Worrying and Start Living*, where we find detailed techniques for controlling ourselves and getting on with our daily routines, this book, *How to Stop Living and Start Worrying*, offers an alternative approach – namely, that in a world defined by ever-growing inequality, political violence, ecological devastation, war and ethnic conflict, there are good reasons to worry; and in a time where death has become the last great taboo, we should revive the philosophical art of dying well: *ars moriendi*.

The book consists of six chapters. Chapter 1 contains a biographical description of Critchley's life: from his early childhood, family background, failures in formal education, the punk scene, through to a serious industrial injury which had huge psychological effects, to the formative years at the University of Essex and finally to life in New York and many other corners of the world.

Critchley's orientation towards philosophy, which he lays out in chapter 2, is one in which the division between philosophy and culture is rejected. For Critchley, philosophy has a radically 'local character' and '*must* form part of the life of a culture'. Philosophy cannot, therefore, be conceived of as a merely professional or academic activity, but a practice that aims to challenge the status quo of the contemporary socio-political situation. This means – and here Critchley turns to Husserl and Heidegger – that the role of the philosopher is to generate 'genealogies which produce crises'. The worst possible situation for a philosopher occurs when a crisis is not recognized. For in such a situation, Critchley argues, 'human beings sink to the level of happy cattle, a sort of bovine contentment that is systematically confused with happiness'.

In chapter 3, which is concerned with the question of death, Critchley begins with Heidegger's claim that death is the 'possibility of impossibility'. For Heidegger, the question of death is a question of *my* death. This is to say that no one can be a substitute for my own death. Critchley turns against this argument, claiming that death comes into life through the death of others. To make this argument, he draws on Blanchot and Levinas, for whom death is the 'impossibility of possibility'. This idea that death is no longer a possibility for the subject is explored in greater detail through the dramas of Ibsen, Racine's *Phaedra* and the work of Beckett. We also find, in this chapter, a long commentary on his bestselling book, *The Book of Dead Philosophers* (2009), which is motivated by Montaigne's well-known line, 'to philosophize is to learn how to die'. While defending the ideal of the philosophical death (up to a certain point), Critchley describes how he has become increasingly sceptical towards its currency.

A question that has run through Critchley's work for a long time, but of which he has remained surprisingly silent until now, is the question of love. In chapter 4, Critchley paints a captivating picture of love by turning to medieval mysticism, including the movement of the free spirit and the fascinating figure of Marguerite Porete, a Beguine mystic who was burned at the stake in 1310 in Paris. For Porete, love is a question that concerns the love of god. In her dramatic language, she says that 'one must hew and hack away at oneself in order to make a space that is large enough for love to enter'. Following Porete, and with a nod to the poet Anne Carson, Critchley suggests that 'love is an act of absolute spiritual daring that eviscerates the old self in order that something new can come into being'. By the end of the chapter, these thoughts are discussed in relation to masochism, possession and female and male sexuality.

Chapter 5 lays out Critchley's theory of humour, which is defined by its ability to change the situation in which we find ourselves: jokes 'tear holes in our usual views of the empirical world'. They allow us to see things in a different light, as in Freud's example, which describes 'a condemned man who, on the morning of his execution, leaves his cell, walks out into the courtyard, sees the gallows ahead of him, sees his fate, looks up at the sky and says: "well, the week's beginning nicely"'. The lesson of this joke is that humour allows us to look upon ourselves, from outside of ourselves, and find ourselves inescapably ridiculous. And this, Critchley argues, is what comic acknowledgement comes down to. The comic subject accepts finitude as a brute fact, but, like the characters in Beckett, keeps moving. Linking comic subjectivity to ethics, Critchley takes this argument to another level, arguing for an ethical subjectivity based on the experience of conscience.

One of the distinctive features of Critchley's work is his interest in collaboration, as is evidenced by his work with the French artist Philippe Parreno and the psychoanalyst Jamieson Webster. The final chapter – chapter 6 – presents a three-way conversation to include Critchley's long-time collaborator Tom McCarthy, the novelist of, among other books, *Remainder* and *Men in Space*. Over the past decade, they have written a number of texts and declarations on the relationship between literature and philosophy. However, it is predominantly through the *International Necronautical Society* (INS) that their collaboration has centred. The INS began as a conceptual art project but has now grown into a semi-fictitious organization, where McCarthy functions as General Secretary and Critchley as Chief Philosopher. In form, it is highly indebted to the historical avant-garde: the futurists and the surrealists all the way up to the situationists. But what separates the INS from these other movements is that it fetishizes, not technology – as the futurists do – but death. As described in McCarthy's first manifesto: 'death is a type of space, which we intend to map, enter, colonise and, eventually, inhabit.' In our conversation, McCarthy explains how, for him, the ultimate question concerns the subject, and the subject's relationship to death. Rather than defending tragic subjectivity, which, in his words, 'pits the self against death in a way that produces authenticity', he defends comic subjectivity, which concerns 'the inability to be oneself, and to become what one wants to be'. Apart from these themes – which mainly revolve around the emergence of the INS and their engagement with philosophy and literature – the conversations also include an assault on neuroscience, post-humanism and what both Critchley and McCarthy see as a regrettable obsession with the future. As Critchley, puzzlingly, put it: 'The future is the enemy of radical thought. It prevents interesting thinking. It's reactionary.'

The idea for this book came out of a television series, broadcasted on Swedish television's TV8, in early 2009. Over four episodes, Critchley and I, together with three invited guests, discussed the nature of philosophy; death; poetry and philosophy; and the relation between science and religion. This book has given us the much-desired opportunity to extend those discussions.

Finally, I would like to thank Emma Hutchinson, John Thompson, Todd Kesselman and Peter Fleming for indispensable editorial work.

Carl Cederström

Life

CARL CEDERSTRÖM: *This interview will focus on your life and how you got into philosophy. But before that I would like to ask a more general question about the relation between philosophy and biography. What can you say about this connection?*

SIMON CRITCHLEY: I think that there's an essential connection between biography and philosophy. The standard version of the history of philosophy begins with Socrates, with a life and a death. It begins with four dialogues by Plato (*Apology*, *Euthyphro*, *Crito* and *Phaedo*), on the trial and execution of Socrates. These dialogues give us a picture of Socrates' life, his teachings and, significantly, the manner of his death at the hands of the Athenian authorities. Philosophy begins with an act of political assassination. We shouldn't forget that. As is clear from a later text like Diogenes Laertius' *Lives and Opinions of Eminent Philosophers*, in the ancient world philosophy had an intimate connection with biography. The biography was a kind of propaedeutic to philosophy. If philosophy was a way of life, then the lives of the philosophers were essential objects of study. You can point to other examples of the way in which biography persists in relation to philosophy all the way up to Spinoza, where, on the one hand, we don't know much about Spinoza's life, but then, in the years after his death, three biographies appeared. He became a sort of atheist saint. And then, with someone like Nietzsche, where the life and the work get confused, where in a sense the life is the work and the work is the life.

CC: *The idea that philosophy cannot be separated from one's life. Is that an idea that would apply also to you, that your life and work have become inseparable?*

SC: Hoist with my own petard, I suppose. The twentieth-century attitude, particularly in the Anglo-American world – but not just in the Anglo-American world – is that philosophy has no relationship to biography. The idea is that philosophical arguments are true by virtue of their form, or by virtue of their proof, or by their ability to be verified, while the facts about the person who wrote those things are of no importance. That's true in Analytic philosophy, but also in Continental philosophy. Heidegger says in a lecture course about Aristotle from the 1920s that he was born, he worked and he died – and that's all we need to know. So there's a real hostility to biography in twentieth-century philosophy, which goes together with a sort of modernist aesthetic, an austerity that tries to separate the truth of the work from one's life. For my part, I think biography is important as a path into philosophy, and also a sort of test of philosophy; and to whether life and work can be integrated. In my case, life and work are completely confused.

CC: *Philosophizing one's life can be done in a variety of ways, of course. On the one hand, it could be a way to protect oneself. It offers a language, and a rather seductive language at that, through which you might externalize yourself, or become detached and distanced. But, on the other hand, it could also be the case that philosophy might be extremely painful, taking you in undesired and embarrassing directions.*

SC: Yeah, the idea is whether philosophy is protection and detachment, or exposure and risk. I think it's both, although it's probably more protective. You see, this is what a lot of philosophy teachers do. They will construct a persona, which seems to be a biographical persona – it seems to be someone they actually are – but really it's just a protective structure. The person they are in public has no relation to who they are. So there's a fake protection of giving oneself a public persona, which has no relation to oneself. But philosophy, or to philosophize, can also be about exposure and risk; and it should be. This exposure can happen in different ways, of course, not least through psychoanalysis.

CC: *At the same time there's this fear to be spoken of, which is perhaps why psychoanalysts like Lacan and Freud burnt manuscripts on a couple of occasions – for fear of what future biographers would do with them. This would be the flip side of psychoanalysis, and maybe also philosophy: the hesitation to symbolize or write oneself. Can you feel this fear of being written?*

SC: What happens, ineluctably and regrettably, is that one becomes a brand: a persona about which various stories, anecdotes and gossip can be circulated. That can ring incredibly hollow and creates I feel, at times, a feeling of utter self-revulsion. Look, I try to be truthful. But I also don't believe we have any privileged intuition into who we are. I don't think introspection produces such great wonders. I think consciousness is a kind of *méconnaisance*, a misrecognition, as Lacan says. What I've learnt from psychoanalysis is that whatever insight I might have into myself is something I normally get from another person; usually and hopefully a person I love. The person you love can tell you something about yourself, from which you can then learn who you are.

CC: *You have jokingly said that you're a critical, secular, well-dressed post-Kantian – would that be your brand?*

SC: No. That was said as a rhetorical ploy in a sort of critical, secular, liberal, post-Kantian context – you know, some of those gorgeous, super-clever, holier-than-thou people you find in New York. I don't think I'm any of those. I'm not particularly critical or even particularly good at criticism. I'm not secular, that's for sure. I have a much more tortured relationship to religion and issues of faith. Maybe I'm post-Kantian, but in a pretty strange way. And I'm not liberal, in any way at all.

CC: *OK. With this in mind, could we perhaps go back in time to speak about you?*

SC: If you insist. I'd rather talk about you.

CC: *But that's not going to happen. We're going to speak about you. Now, I don't know much about your childhood. The only thing that you've mentioned is that you were in a school with 11-year-old boys with beards and that you, in order to escape all the violence, had to perform exceptionally well so that you could get into another school. And this was in Liverpool?*

SC: No, my family is from Liverpool, but I grew up in Letchworth Garden City, 30 miles north of London, in Hertfordshire, affectionately known as the wasteland.

CC: *What kind of place was that?*

SC: A wasteland, like I said. It was built as a Quaker socialist utopia in 1900. It was a project called Garden Cities – really interesting idea – with a tree outside every house, social housing and all the rest. My dad, Bill Critchley, left Liverpool in the '50s because there was no work. He came south, and then the family came after him – basically, economic migration. The usual story. My dad was a sheet-metal worker, and my mother, Sheila, who had worked as a hairdresser in Liverpool, was home looking after my sister, who is six years older than me. As a sheet-metal worker, a rented house came with the job. He worked very hard and he did well and he was promoted. And when I was 8 years old we bought a house – which was a big deal – and we moved to the other side of town. So we moved from what was a very working-class area to a more middle-class area. And I changed schools. I went to the local school around the corner and then the local public primary school, as they're called in England.

CC: *So how did you experience school? Were you considered a good student?*

SC: Yes. I did really well in school at that point. At the age of 5, 6, 7 I was really good – top of the class. But then we moved and I started a new school where I got bullied, for maybe two years. It was horrible. I was around 9, 10 at the time – it was an awful period – and I remember that I refused to go to school because I was so terrified of being beaten up. But what saved me was football. I could play football and it is still maybe the governing passion of my life. My only religious commitment is to Liverpool Football Club. My dad had been trained at the Liverpool ground and he had taught me. He stopped playing because of an ankle injury. I was pretty good for a kid from Letchworth. I was fast and I was big. And I got onto the school team and the county team. Only two kids from my school got onto the county team – this was a big deal. So suddenly, at 10 years old, I had a lot of respect. So football saved my life. I still got beaten up, and I got beaten up for the way I spoke. So I changed the way I spoke overnight and lost my Liverpool accent for this entirely bland way I speak now. I don't know how much violence there is now, with kids.

CC: *Quite a lot I imagine, especially here in London.*

SC: I remember an awful lot of violence and I got beaten up regularly. But basically, to go back to your question, it was the fear of physical violence that focused my mind on school. This is true – you'd think I was making this shit up – but it's actually true: my teacher in school, in the final year of primary school, found me and two other boys, jumping on desks and making noise – we were 10 years old. And this man, a grown-up man in his thirties, dragged us out of the classroom and hit all of us until we fell over. Seriously, he beat us to the ground. And we just took it. Eventually, weeks later, we complained to our parents, who then complained to the school, and he was dismissed the following year. I saw him driving a cab some years later.

CC: *So you were working hard to escape the violence, both from teachers and violent 10-year-olds with beards?*

SC: Yes. And in those days it was a very simple system. You knew exactly where you were in the hierarchy. The top ten students from the primary school got into the grammar school, and the grammar school was an academic school, which meant that there were no big men with beards and your face wasn't pushed down the toilet everyday (who knows, psychoanalytically understood, maybe this was what I secretly desired). So through this fear of going to what was then called the secondary modern school, where 90 per cent of the population went, I realized I had to work. So I worked my way up to the first table and passed the entrance exam, what was called at the time the '11 plus'.

CC: *So you made it. How was grammar school?*

SC: We were taught by these very old men who wore gowns, and they were very ferocious. We did Latin, ancient history, sciences, languages (French and Russian) and English literature. There was an ancient history teacher who had a huge impact on me. We just did ancient history for two years and I became obsessed with it. Still am. I still have a book from those days, because I stole it from the library. It's called *Everyday Life in Babylon and Assyria*. A real page-turner. I read this when I was 11 years old. It was wonderful. I read about the ancient world, Mesopotamian culture, Sumerian, Babylonian, Assyrian and then the Greeks. I was reading books – very simple ones like Kitto's book *The Greeks* – on ancient history and that captivated me. When I did philosophy 11 years later I already had an attraction to Greek philosophy for that reason. What interested me about ancient history was the fact that it bore no relation to reality. It seemed to be a complete fantasy world. When history became real, I remember when we got to medieval history and then early modern history I entirely lost interest.

CC: *How about your parents, were they supportive in your ambitions?*

SC: My parents were great, but they had no particular interest in my education. They were encouraging at certain moments, but for the most part they were neutral. I was at a grammar school, and I think they were pleased, but I certainly wasn't pushed. And then when I went to university, when I was 22, in October 1982, I was actually discouraged very strongly by my parents; they thought it was a completely ludicrous idea. Ours was not an educated family and I was the first one that went beyond 16. My father and mother left school when they were 14.

CC: *So it was not your parents who pushed you in the direction of becoming a philosopher?*

SC: Oh no. My father would have been delighted if I'd worked in a factory, and my mother would've been ecstatic if I'd worked in a bank, because that's a good job – what could be better than that? The other important thing about these years was that my mother and father split up. I was 14 at the time, although it had been in the air for at least the three previous years. My father had a succession of affairs and then ended up leaving my mother for his secretary – a depressingly predictable scenario. My sister got married when I was 14, and that turned out to be the last time I saw my whole extended Liverpool family together for many years – which was a pity because we'd been really close.

CC: *And how did you react to the divorce?*

SC: Badly. After the divorce, I did catastrophically at school. I went from being a pretty good student to failing all my O-levels at 16, which is this qualification that you needed to get in order to go on to A-levels and then university. I failed them in a spirit of wilful self-destruction. I left formal education at the age of 16 with one 'C' grade in geography. I've always loved maps. I remember that I went to the pub after everybody else got their results. Everybody had done a lot better than me. And it then hit me that maybe I had made a huge mistake, because I deliberately failed them. I thought education was ridiculous. At that point I was into progressive German music like Can, Neu!, Kraftwerk and Tangerine Dream (the first band I saw live when I was 14) – these were the only things that were really important to me. To get some money to survive over the summer, my best friend Russell and I signed on the dole. It felt great. I then went to a catering technical college, which was a further education college for people learning to become welders and hairdressers or whatever. It wasn't exactly a great place, but it was next to the school. In fact, my old school was closed and turned into an unemployment benefit office and the catering technical college was demolished and replaced by a supermarket –

that's progress! So I was at catering technical college for two years, which was an absolute disaster. I had no interest in it at all. I was playing in all these bands, and then punk happened, in winter 1976. Year zero!

CC: *Punk has obviously had a huge impact on your life – and you often return to the theme in your work. In* Very Little . . . Almost Nothing, *for example, you describe punk as 'acting like an oxygen tank for those being suffocated for what passes for life in English suburbia'. Can you describe that moment when punk happened?*

SC: Punk happened really fast. It was a transcendent moment. I remember hearing the first Ramones album, at a friend's house very late at night and 'drunk', as it were. Suddenly it was as if every record I had heard – and all that mattered to me, as a kid, was listening to music and buying albums – had been erased. And then all these bands entered the scene, like, *The Damned*, *The Buzzcocks* and, obviously, *The Sex Pistols* and *The Clash*. But I also loved lesser-known bands like *The Vibrators*, *The Only Ones* and *The Radiators from Outer Space*. And also *Wire*. I still love *Wire*, especially 'Outdoor Miner'. It was that feeling of being part of something magical: that London was the centre of the world. Crucially, a lot of punk was not by Londoners: it was by kids out in the suburbs, in the wasteland, places like Bromley, who identified with London as a magical place. This is 1976–7, and I was a big-time punk, with bondage trousers, ten-hole Dr Martens boots and a Lewis leather jacket.

CC: *But we both know that you didn't become a rock star, but a philosopher. So what happened?*

SC: What happened was that I had an industrial accident – and this is really important. It was in September 1978, and I was working in a pharmaceutical factory in Hitchin, where my mum and I moved early in 1978, because we had to sell the house. I was taking out powder from a machine, in which you had metal paddles, about an inch thick, mixing the drugs. And in order to get all the powder out you had to reach into the machine with your hand and push it all down into the hole, at which point some fucking idiot turned on the machine and my hand was trapped inside it. I remember that Jilted John's first single was on the radio. I literally had to bend the paddles to pull my hand out of the machine. All the bones were smashed and the tendons severed. I was in hospital for two weeks and then had to go through three operations. Skin grafts, reconstructive surgery. The whole banana. After two weeks, I was told by the doctor that I could keep my hand. Until that time I had no idea that I could have lost it. But the hand was so badly damaged they were expecting it to rot. Funnily enough, I'm registered disabled because of the hand. I have a 15 per cent impairment. I can't make a fist, for example. Sort of symbolic. So, I'm 18 years old and the only things I enjoy are playing guitar and writing songs. And my left hand is my guitar hand, so I thought I could never play guitar again. I went into a massive depression, the whole of that winter, for six, seven months. And to overcome the depression I did an awful lot of drugs. But then, of course, you get even more depressed. I was going to London a lot at this time, hanging out with the wrong people, drug-dealers and the like. I still had this ambition of playing in bands, switched over to keyboards and then discovered I could still play guitar, but in a different way, I had to relearn the whole thing and then carried on with a failed musical career.

CC: *This was a life-changing event?*

SC: Yes, and I think it could be helpful to intellectualize this a little. Sartre has this idea of a radical project. It's part of his critique of Freudian psychoanalysis, where everything is meant to happen in the infantile stage. Sartre's idea is that there can be a fundamental project, or a radical project, where one makes a choice at a certain age. He's thinking of Jean Genet who makes the choice of being a thief, at the age of 14, when he is discovered stealing and someone calls him a thief and he accepts it, saying 'OK, I'm a thief'. So for me, there was punk first and then this industrial injury, which was a sort of break in my existence. Oh, I also had another industrial injury where I lost part of my finger when I was 14. I learned that I should stay away from factories. The trauma also had the effect of erasing big chunks of memory – I was wiped clean. As a result, I have very poor memory of my childhood. So, there I was, at the age of 18, with no memory and no real basis to life, still living in the wasteland.

CC: *So what did you do?*

SC: I started working as a lifeguard, for about 16 months. I'm not joking. I was a good swimmer. Now, the only thing you're not allowed to do when you're at a swimming pool was to read. So, I started to read. Thousands of children drowned as a result.

CC: *What were you reading?*

SC: I read Aldous Huxley, George Orwell – all of it – and then I migrated into *Penguin Modern Classics*: Nietzsche, Camus, Sartre. Then I discovered Burroughs, Bataille, things like that.

CC: *And you had not been reading a lot until this point?*

SC: No, at least not in a serious way. So, I was about 20 and decided to go to a further education college in Stevenage, which was not a great place. But I could do it and claim unemployment benefit, so it was cool. I stayed there for two years, between 20 and 22. I initially did O-levels, which means I did what you usually do when you are 16 when I was 20 or 21. Sort of humiliating. The problem was that I couldn't physically write because of my injury (I'm left-handed). So I had to relearn how to write, which I still have difficulties with. It involves a great deal of pain. Maybe that's important. Anyhow, I did two A-levels in the second year. I did English literature and some nonsense called 'Communication Studies'. I discovered T. S. Eliot, and a lot of other poets as well, people like Donne and Marvell. I taught myself Middle English; learnt to read Chaucer and Piers Plowman in Middle English. I still love Middle English – it comes in very useful in New York. Coming from the wasteland, I became obsessed by Eliot's 'The Waste Land'; read Joyce's *Ulysses*; read Kafka, Camus, Beckett. I was reading the standard European avant-garde modernist canon. In the second year at the further education college I had no money – I was doing all sorts of jobs on the side to support myself – and in the library one day someone said I should apply to university. It had never crossed my mind before. I was 21 years old. It took a long time to do anything with that thought. But I eventually applied to the University of Essex where I was admitted to do philosophy and literature. But when I got there I immediately changed to do English and European literature and they didn't mind me doing that. This was 1982. I was 22 years old, all of a sudden at university. I had received a grant because my mother had no money and I could even claim travel expenses. Heaven.

CC: *Essex was a really radical and interesting campus at that time.*

SC: Yes, it had been through this extraordinary period of the 1970s and I was arriving at the fag end of that whole thing. But it was still a very interesting place to be. All the students were 18 or 19. So I was three years older than the students, which was cool, because I had done all the stuff that they were trying to do – and I could still be cool, because I looked cool, with stupid dyed blonde hair and dressed in whatever I was able to find.

CC: *How much did you know about Essex before you arrived?*

SC: Absolutely nothing. I didn't know where it was – I didn't even know what a university was.

CC: *So it was just pure luck?*

SC: Pure luck. I travelled to three universities, and to my surprise I got into them all: Essex, Sussex and Warwick. I chose Essex because I could do straight literature, but also because I wanted to go to a left-wing university. My politics throughout this period was very left wing. Most of my friends were extremely racist, and reactionary to say the least. But I never was. My dad used to call himself a communist when I was 12, 13, 14. I was very impressed by the Soviet Union at that time. He ended up voting for Thatcher in 1983 and we fought like cats and dogs about the miners' strike in 1984–5.

CC: *And how did you fit in with the rest of the students?*

SC: I was hugely intimidated, because these were the kind of middle-class kids I had never really met before. I was repulsed by most of them. I thought they were pathetic. Posers. The highest form of abuse for a punk is to be a poser, rather than being a real punk. And I thought they were posers. Nobody from my circle in bands or whatever – nobody went to university – so I had the feeling of being in the wrong place. I even had a breakdown in my first year of university, because I thought, 'this is beyond me'. I had the feeling of being a fraud and that someone would find that out. I really pushed myself to get through the first year. Then at the end of my first year, I came in second out of 300 students, in my exams. I had gone back to Hitchin after the exams so it was not until I got back to campus that I found out. People came up and congratulated me and I got this award or whatever. I was astonished. Once that happened I was identified as a bright student and really encouraged by some brilliant teachers like Jay Bernstein, Robert Bernasconi, Ludmilla Jordanova, Onora O'Neill, Frank Cioffi, Mike Weston, Roger Moss and Gabriel Pearson. I then switched to philosophy because the philosophy teachers were just much better. I ended up getting a first class degree, which was what you needed to get the money to do graduate work

CC: *Could you say something about the climate at Essex at that time?*

SC: It was amazing. I joined the Communist Students' Society, and this is where I first read Althusser, Foucault, Derrida. And the Communist Students' Society was closely linked to the Black Students' Alliance. Imagine these seminar rooms at Essex, out in the fields, filled with Marxists from Nigeria and from central Africa, discussing the nature of ideology and class struggle. For me it was hypnotizing. I was also involved in the Poetry Society there, although I realized that I wasn't a very good poet. I stopped writing poetry when I was 25, after reading W. H. Auden. But I left Essex when I was 25 and I was with a woman named Anthea – we were together for many years – and we moved to France. The idea was to take the money from my first class degree, move to France, and never come back. We had this romantic idea of living in the south of France. But it was a complicated hell. Anthea couldn't get a job. We had very little money. It was really tough. And I hated Nice.

CC: *But it was in Nice that you met Dominique Janicaud?*

SC: That's right. He was my teacher and for no reason at all he was very kind to me. He taught me how to do research. I learnt how to use a library and how to really write. I had been a good student and done well. But it was in France where it really got serious. I realized that there were things I wanted to say. And I learnt French properly. I wrote a thesis in French, on Heidegger and Carnap, on the question of the overcoming of metaphysics. I had wonderful teachers, like Janicaud, Clement Rosset and André Tosel.

CC: *And you returned to Essex to finish your PhD thesis?*

SC: Yes. I stayed in France for a year and a half. So when I got back to Essex there were only 16 months left, and I had no PhD topic. Absolutely none. But I realized I had grown up a lot in France. I seemed to be moving at a different pace from many of the other graduate students (there were only about 10 graduate students in philosophy at Essex at the time). I ended up doing a PhD in less than a year on Derrida and Levinas; that was the basis for my first book, *The Ethics of Deconstruction*.

CC: *Were you aiming for an academic position already then?*

SC: No, not at all. There were no jobs in academia, so it wasn't even an ambition. People forget this, but between 1977 and 1988, first under Labour and then under Thatcher and the Tories, there were no academic jobs, especially in the Humanities. This is why there's a missing generation in the UK. None of the graduate students at Essex expected to get jobs. In my third and final year as a PhD student, Christopher Norris came to Essex and mentioned that I should come along to Cardiff. I gave my first paper in February 1988 and

I was terrified. Amazingly, Cardiff offered me a decently paid postdoctoral fellowship the next month, and the talk I gave was published, my first real publication. Thinking back it's really strange: I was 22 years old, did my BA, Master's and PhD in six years and then had a paid job at 28. At the same time my PhD supervisor, Robert Bernasconi, was leaving Essex. There's a long story attached to this, which I have never really got to the bottom of. But they wanted me to apply for this job and they offered it to me. They appointed Peter Dews and myself to the Essex department on the same day. And it was absolutely astonishing. I went to Cardiff for a rain-soaked, beer-and-meat-pie-sodden year where I learnt a lot. Taught a course on philosophical aesthetics and read a lot of Kant, Benjamin, Lacan and Paul de Man.

CC: *That's a lot of things happening within the course of only six or seven years. So this was the 'radical project' that followed from the industrial injury?*

SC: Yes. The injury recalibrated my entire organism. I became a different person; some people say that I changed dramatically. Obviously, I can't judge. Another important thing was that I had problems with my ears; everyone in my family has had problems with their ears. When I was 25 I went to get my ears syringed in Nice, and they fucked it up in some way and I got tinnitus: constant ringing in the ears, which I still have, 25 years later. It's unbearable at times. The first couple of years I felt suicidal. What I decided – in my perversity – when I was about 26, was that I was never going to be happy because of this ringing in my ears. There's nothing worse. It's as if someone is inside your head. I also had terrible insomnia for a long period of time. It was this sense of being alone at night with this noise that you can't switch off. Absolutely unbearable. The only thing I could really do was to work and study, to read and write. Particularly write. Writing seemed to make the pain go away, it made the noise go away. Given that I'm not going to be happy or contented, or to lead a nice life – this is how naive I was – I said to myself that I will try and study philosophy in a way that would help people who were in the same situation as I was when I first started studying. I was reading Heidegger's description of anxiety when I was about 23, where anxiety reveals the nothing: that rare mood where everything retreats to inexistence and insignificance. The world is just a chaos of meaninglessness, and the self precipitates at this nothingness which faces this world. So that feeling of a classical existential mood, made absolute sense to me.

CC: *So you're now 29 years old and have a job in the philosophy department at Essex. And then your book,* The Ethics of Deconstruction, *came out, which became a great success. Could you say something about that?*

SC: *The Ethics of Deconstruction* was finished in September 1991, and published the following May. And then the Derrida scandal broke. Derrida was initially denied an honorary doctorate at Cambridge. He was suddenly front-page news and the status of this weird thing called 'deconstruction' was a topic of public debate. I remember a headline from May 1992 – from the *Independent* newspaper I think – which read: 'Value-Free Nihilism Hits English City'. That was the day after it was finally decided to offer Derrida the doctorate, following opposition from most members of the philosophy department at Cambridge. The issue was whether deconstruction was nihilism, you know, undermining all that is important in Western civilization [yawn]. It just so happened that I had written a book arguing that deconstruction had to be understood as an ethical project in Levinas's sense and that it had significant political consequences. So it sold a lot and the book was everywhere. Sheer good luck. It couldn't have been planned.

CC: *One could almost suspect you for being the mastermind behind the Cambridge scandal.*

SC: I wish I had been. So, suddenly I had a successful book and I was projected into a different sort of world. I started to travel around to give talks. Going to the United States a lot and to Paris, all over. It felt very glamorous, wonderful and, of course, filled me with self-doubt and disgust. What I became convinced of was the idea that I had to do something that was not the same book. Writing a first book is hard enough. And getting the fucking thing read is enormously difficult. But if you're lucky enough to get to that stage, then what do you do? Do you just repeat the thing? You just write *The Ethics of Deconstruction 2.0*? I didn't want to do that, so I decided to do something absolutely different. I began thinking of going down a different path – this was in 1993. I had been drawn to the work of Maurice Blanchot for many years. The first book I read, cover to cover, in French, was his *L'Espace littéraire* [*The Space of Literature*]. His French was utterly limpid. At the same time I was greatly influenced by Jay Bernstein at this point. He was in the office next door to me and the best philosophical interlocutor. He still is. Jay's work is very much animated by the question of nihilism, and I really took on this question in a different way from him. And I then began writing the book *Very Little . . . Almost Nothing*, which was finished four years later. I remember, at the time, people thinking I was crazy, publishing a book like this, at this time, with such a silly title. I remember someone telling me: 'This is a suicide note.'

CC: *But in a way you had already done it. The thesis you wrote in Nice, on Heidegger and Carnap, was very different from your PhD.*

SC: You just have to keep moving. It is a question of maintaining a curiosity and a hunger and also an absolute self-doubt about what you're up to. T. S. Eliot has this line where he says that writing is about mastering tools, which, once mastered, are useless. Once you have learnt to write something, you can no longer redo it. You have to learn a new skill every time. And every book I've done is an attempt to master something, that when mastered becomes irrelevant.

CC: *To go back to* Very Little . . . Almost Nothing, *how would you describe that book?*

SC: It is more of a cult book, sort of a second album. It comes out of a very obvious and profound experience, which is that of my father's death – my dad died of lung cancer between Christmas and New Year, in 1994. I split up from my long-time partner, Anthea, around the same time. When I found out my father was terminally ill, my life seemed to turn upside down. I remember sitting downstairs at my dad's house, taking a break from helping to nurse him with my mother and sister, and reading Beckett's *Malone Dies*. It didn't make obvious sense at the time. Around this time there were other tracks I was following. I began to formulate this idea of philosophy beginning in disappointment, the two main forms of disappointment being political and religious. And these two axes became a good way to describe around what my work was circulating during the 1990s. So the book came out when I was living in Frankfurt and again nothing really happened, no reviews appeared. It felt like a mistake. It was a book that has had a much more interesting and lively after-life than immediate effect. There are people out there that still see me as the author of *Ethics of Deconstruction* and there are those who see me as the author of *Very Little . . . Almost Nothing*. I think I prefer the latter bunch.

CC: *But your next book,* Ethics–Politics–Subjectivity, *which came out in 1999, was not entirely different from what you had been doing. Could you say something about that book?*

SC: I was working a lot with Ernesto Laclau at that time, and he picked up the arguments of *The Ethics of Deconstruction*. And I began to refine and develop the arguments about ethics and politics that I initially developed in *The Ethics of Deconstruction*. I disagreed with myself in certain fundamental regards. I was trying to develop a much more coherent political position. And then I was suddenly in these debates with Ernesto Laclau, Richard Rorty and Jacques Derrida. It didn't make any sense to me at the time and it doesn't make any sense now. *Ethics–Politics–Subjectivity* is my German book, written in libraries in Frankfurt for the most part. It also shows the extent of my engagement with psychoanalysis, which was something I had learnt from my partner at the time, Cecilia Sjöholm. Next, I began to write *Continental Philosophy*, which Oxford University Press asked me to write. They wanted me to write an introductory book. It was not so much an introductory book. It was, rather, my meta-philosophical account of how I see the discipline of philosophy and its cultural function. I finished the Continental philosophy book in Sydney and then, around the same time, I was writing a book called *On Humour* for Tony Bruce at Routledge, who's been a good friend over the years. The idea was to write a 30,000-word intervention book, the sort of thing that everyone is doing now, but they were not that common at the time. Sometimes, I think that *On Humour* is my best book; sometimes, I don't know.

CC: *It is also a book that marks a great shift in tone. You're writing much more accessibly.*

SC: Yes, I begin to develop a different sensibility. Writing the introductory book meant I had to communicate in a different way. And I quite liked it. I found that I was able to pitch things in a different way, for a bigger audience. The humour book I particularly liked because even if you know relatively little about philosophy, you can pick that book up and make sense of it. If you know a lot you can detect all sorts of background landscapes and figures moving behind the curtains, and I rather like that.

CC: *And then there's your short book on poetry.*

SC: Yes, on Wallace Stevens. An obsession of mine. I wanted to write a small book on why I thought that reading poetry mattered philosophically. Very simple idea. It has ideas in it that I still use and the last, long chapter on Stevens's late poetry is important to me. I've tried to continue in this vein in some unpublished work on Ponge and Pessoa. Although this hasn't really been picked up on, *Things Merely Are* is the closest I get to dealing with epistemological issues and disappointment with regard to knowledge – what I call 'dejected transcendental idealism'.

CC: *Your next book,* Infinitely Demanding, *returns to some of your early thoughts on ethics, but you approach the subject very differently.*

SC: I was at a conference in about 2000 and I had to present the argument of *Ethics–Politics–Subjectivity* and realized that I didn't really know what the argument was. I couldn't really articulate it, so I began to step back and really think about metaethics, what are the sources and nature of normativity. And I began to develop an idea of a grammar of practical reason, based on a theory of approval and demand, which is taken from an essay by a German philosopher called Dieter Henrich, whom I had been reading in those years. Then I gave a course on the concept of commitment in about 2001, at Essex. And at the same point, Seattle had happened: the anti-globalization movement had begun to take shape. Students were becoming radicalized in a different way. In

Essex, the way it happened was that a lot of students around Ernesto Laclau were dissatisfied with the discourse theory framework, disco-Marxism as it were, and they wanted to go back to Marx and engage with the critique of political economy, questions of class and revolutionary change. We had a reading group at Essex – I think it was called a radical politics reading group – and I was reading Marx with PhD students, and began thinking about politics in different ways. And I was trying to make sense of what was happening with the radical politics in those years. Books like *Empire* [Negri and Hardt] were being published, and there seemed to be a different mood in the air. Also, I'd been reading Alain Badiou's work from about 1994–5, and then developed a friendship with Badiou in the late '90s; he had an influence over the way in which I think and write. I decided to write in a much more systematic and concise conceptual way, and not to do so much commentary and exegesis – all of those elements came together in what became *Infinitely Demanding*. Prima facie, it's a very short book. It's only about 150 pages. But there are an awful lot of arguments in it, and it took a lot of time to formulate, particularly the chapter on politics, which goes from Marx all the way through the anarchist position that I've been trying to defend in recent years.

CC: *And it was around this time that you left Essex and moved to New York. What motivated that move?*

SC: What was happening in these years was an increasing dissatisfaction with Britain. In the early 1990s there was a really interesting intellectual context. There were people like Gillian Rose, David Wood, Jay Bernstein and Geoff Bennington – there was a very high level of intellectual activity. And really good younger people, like Howard Caygill, Peter Osborne, Keith Ansell Pearson, Nick Land and many others. People were really pushing the envelope, thinking hard about deep issues and the standard was extremely high. The graduate students at Essex in those years were very good. They all had second languages and worked like dogs. But then it began to fall apart under the middle management takeover of British academia that has happened over the past 15 years or so. To be honest, I was only staying in Essex to spend more time with my son, Edward, and I realized that it was no longer the place it used to be. People either retired, died, left for the US or stopped doing interesting work. Somehow, I had become 'Mr Continental Philosophy' in the UK and I hated it because it was stupid. I was getting a lot of gigs with the BBC and writing quasi-journalistic pieces, but it was all pretty anodyne and low level. I didn't feel there was anything demanding, as it were. And the graduate students were an awful lot worse than they used to be. So I went to New York in 2004, which was a fantastic opportunity. I knew about the myth of the New School and had read Arendt, Jonas and Schürmann. The fact is that when I got there in 2004 it was a real jolt, because I had to perform on a much higher level than I did at Essex. I had to improve my teaching significantly, change gear and generally push much harder. I had become lazy in my last years in Britain.

CC: *You then went to Los Angeles for a year, as a scholar at the Getty Research Institute.*

SC: Don't remind me! I got a Getty Trust fellowship to work on a project in relation to religion. I had been teaching a course on Rousseau for a couple of years at the New School and wrote this long essay called *Catechism of the Citizen* on the relation between politics and religion in Rousseau. It came out as a little book in German and will form part of my next book, called *The Faith of the Faithless*, which is about political theology. I was then talking to George Miller, who was an editor at Granta with whom I had been working for some years. We had a drunken lunch in London where we came up with the idea to write a book on how philosophers die. I had time on my hands, in Los Angeles, the city of death, the city of angels. I began to investigate the topic, using the amazing library resources at the Getty and UCLA and discovered this wealth of material. After getting the format and framework of the book clear as *The Book of Dead Philosophers*, it more or less wrote itself. But it was tough, as I was trying to cover the entire history of philosophy, philosopher by philosopher.

CC: *A lot of work?*

SC: Huge amount of work. Writing books is a mug's game. Publishers don't understand – because they don't write books; editors don't understand: they think books grow on trees or something. It's fucking hard work writing books. It demands every fibre of your commitment and being. It's painful. That said, *The Book of Dead Philosophers* was about as much fun as I am ever going to have writing a book. It's a strange book, which is essentially an attempt to reconceive the way we approach the history of philosophy and the activity of philosophy itself. Around the same time, I started putting together this book on Heidegger.

CC: *Which again is a great contrast to the former book. Your most detailed academic engagement since* Very Little . . . Almost Nothing.

SC: Maybe. It is, for the most part, a painstaking scholarly work on Heidegger, which I think is a little constipated as I was taught by Heideggerians and have super-ego problems with the diminutive Schwarzwald Nazi.

CC: *Clearly, you have explored a wide array of topics. So from where do these ideas usually derive?*

SC: It is usually someone else's idea. I think every book has been someone else's idea. Seriously. I don't trust myself, but I am perfectly happy to steal ideas from others.

CC: *Do you find it pleasurable to write?*

SC: Depends. It's generally painful. Sometimes it can be lighter. Sometimes it can even be a delight. When I was writing *Very Little . . . Almost Nothing* I remember talking to people about an almost mystical sense of writing, where the text is writing itself, and you have to attend to it. I still believe that in a way. All you have to do is to sit in front of your computer long enough and the thing will be finished. But, as Pascal said, it is very difficult to remain sitting in a room, reading and writing.

CC: *You have received some criticism over the years. Is this some-thing that affects you?*

SC: Let me go back to an early question about whether phi-losophy is protection or exposure. I try and expose myself in writing. At times, it doesn't add up. I know there are contra-dictions in some of the things I've said. I'm very well aware of that. I sometimes follow a line simply because it interests me. Thank God I still have this extraordinary curiosity about things. And I can still be completely blown away by reading a book, listening to a talk or something that a student says. There's no, as it were, morality in writing. There's an expo-sure and a logic that draws you on. One hopes that it all adds up. Looking back at what I've written over the past 20 years, it is difficult not to feel alienation and nausea. Writing is exposure and readers can be merciless. Criticisms do sting, and what people have said about me over the years – positive and negative – has had an effect. Sure. You can't isolate your-self from that, but nor can you refuse to expose yourself. I've done some pretty stupid things over the years in the name of whatever – vanity and curiosity – but there we are. You throw a lot of shit on the wall and some of it sticks. My worry about philosophers is that they are constipated and that they refuse to take a dump.

CC: *Finally, and this is related to your work at a more general level, I see two movements in your work: one towards youth, where philosophy is the experience of a youthful exhilaration; and one where philosophy is, in Stanley Cavell's words, education for grown-ups.*

SC: It's both things. A permanent strange adolescence or 'adultescence'. I'm still doing the same thing I was doing in my mid-twenties. I'm writing stuff down. I have a better computer now, but essentially it's the same thing. On one level, my life is an infinitely extended childhood, writing philosophy, and I'm surrounded on a daily basis at work by those who are younger than me – like yourself, Carl. I have an implicit trust in what students are reading and what they're interested in. If my anarchist students in New York are taking up Marcuse, I instantly begin to think that maybe I should read Marcuse again. I'm constantly listening to what they're reading. And I try and read with them. If they give me texts, I read them, so there's this vampire side to me where I'm trying to draw the blood out of them. This is of course only one side, about philosophy, a ridiculously extended adolescence. And then you have the other side: philosophy as being preoccupied with death, dying and all the rest. I guess we'll come to that later.

Philosophy

CARL CEDERSTRÖM: *I would like to start this chapter with the most obvious question, which is the question that philosophy has asked itself from the beginning – namely, 'What is philosophy?'*

SIMON CRITCHLEY: The first thing to say is that philosophy is not a solely professional or academic activity for me. Philosophy is not a thing, it's not an entity; it's an activity. To put it tautologically: philosophy is the activity of philosophizing, an activity which is conducted by finite, thinking creatures like us. Now, my general view of philosophy is that this activity *must* form part of the life of a culture. Philosophy is the living activity of critical reflection in a specific context; it always has a radically local character. The way in which philosophy will take place depends on where the questions are asked. So the activity of philosophy is critical reflection in a specific context where human beings are asked to raise questions of a general form, or a universal form. For example, the questions we find Socrates asking in the Platonic dialogues: what is knowledge? what is justice? what is love? and the rest. Philosophy begins with the person of Socrates, but it is already happening amongst the pre-Socratics – in Heraclitus – when common sense or what the Greeks called *doxa* – what passes for common knowledge in a specific place – when *doxa* is pressed and assessed by raising questions of a universal form: what is *x*? To go back to Heraclitus. Heraclitus insisted that the people of Ephesus – where he lived – should follow the logos (you can translate it as *ratio* or reason, but it could also mean Being, in a much broader sense). They should follow the logos, the universal principle, and not be distracted by particular things. And he became so depressed with the citizens of Ephesus that he left and wandered in the countryside and eventually met an unsavoury end, suffocating in cow dung. But the hope that drives the activity of philosophy is that, by raising universal questions, philosophy can challenge what passes for *doxa* in a specific context, and through the activity of argument the pursuit of these questions can have an educative, emancipatory effect. To summarize: philosophy is this activity of critical reflection in a specific context, which has an emancipatory effect. Or the way in which Cavell puts it: philosophy is the education of grown-ups. Philosophy is what adults need in order to become educated.

CC: *To pick up on the question of emancipation, which you claim to be one of the three themes that characterize what we broadly call 'Continental philosophy' (the other two being critique and praxis), could you perhaps say something about this particular approach to philosophy and why it is so important to you?*

SC: Well, I want to get to the question of finitude by looking at what is specific to the Continental approach to philosophy. And I want to do that by addressing a theme, which we can call the theme of history or historicity. Now, unlike much of the Analytic tradition in philosophy, in figures like the early Wittgenstein, where philosophy is expressed in a sort of austere, anti-historical modernism; or indeed, in a philosopher like Quine, where that austerity becomes a form of naturalism; I take it that the Continental tradition in philosophy would refuse the validity of the distinction between philosophy and the history of philosophy. We simply cannot make that distinction. This is why the focus on philosophy in and after Kant is so important, and so important to what people like me try to do; it's after Kant that the question of historicity really becomes central. We find this in the work of thinkers like Hamann, Herder and, most obviously, Hegel. But to go back to your question: what is specific and powerful about the Continental tradition in philosophy is the focus on the essentially historical nature of philosophy, and the essentially historical nature of the philosopher who engages in this practice. And that's the insight into what is normally called *historicity*. So philosophy is an activity of raising questions of a universal form in a specific context; it's an activity defined by historicity. Now, this insight into historicity has the consequence that deep metaphysical questions, about the meaning and value of human life, can no longer simply be referred to the traditional topics of speculative metaphysics – the topics of God, freedom, immortality, the nature of things-in-themselves. These are topics about which Kant, in the *Critique of Pure Reason*, says are cognitively meaningless, although – and this is the argument developed in the second critique, the *Critique of Practical Reason* – they are morally defensible.

CC: *Kant is obviously very central to your work. In* Infinitely Demanding, *for example, you suggest that if you were to give a date and time to your orientation to philosophy – what you call a modern conception of philosophy, beginning in disappointment instead of wonder – then it would be the conception of philosophy that follows from Kant's Copernican revolution. Could you say something more about Kant's importance?*

SC: It's twofold for me. Post-Kantian philosophy introduces two vital themes: *finitude and contingency*. Let me begin with finitude – and this will be the link into the question of death. The post-Kantian tradition begins from the acceptance of the radical finitude of the human subject, self or person – namely, that there is no God-like standpoint or point of reference outside human experience, from which human experience might be characterized or judged. We cannot take a God's eye view on the nature of reality. Kant leaves open the possibility that there might be such a reality, but we can know nothing about it. So the first point is the radical finitude of the human subject. The second essential gain produced by this critical recognition of historicity is contingency. That's to say: human experience is constitutively contingent, or created. Human experience is all-too-human. It's made and remade by us. And the circumstances of the fabrication of human experience are, by definition, contingent, even if – and this is arguably always the case – that contingency feels necessary. The world that we inhabit at any particular point feels like a necessary world: it is structured and ordered in a way that we find compelling. This is the way the world is. But the gain of what happens to philosophy after Kant is the recognition that the world and human experience are contingently articulated. When those two moves have been made – once the human being has been located as a finite subject, embedded in a contingent network of history, culture and society – then one can begin to understand the feature that is common to many philosophers in the Continental tradition, namely the demand that things might be otherwise. If human experience is a contingent creation of finite subjects, then that human experience can be recreated in other ways. What happens after Kant is that, in different forms, we see the articulation of a demand for a transformative practice of philosophy – a practice of philosophy that would be capable of addressing, criticizing and ultimately transforming the present – transforming the world in which we live. The demand that runs through much continental thought is that human beings emancipate themselves from their current conditions, which are conditions not amenable to freedom.

CC: *And this is what you find in someone like Rousseau – another philosopher of major importance for your work – that what defines society is social injustice and inequality.*

SC: Yes, this is the Rousseauesque insight that we find at the beginning of the *Social Contract*, where Rousseau says: 'Man was born free, and he is everywhere in chains.' So the awareness of our contingency is the awareness of the historical formation of a world, a world that enchains us; in Rousseau's words, a world defined by inequality – and this is also why Rousseau is so important to me and to the way I approach philosophy. What Rousseau gives us, in the Second Discourse, the *Discourse on Inequality*, is a genealogy of inequality, describing the way in which human beings have created a world that culminates in a state of war. The insight into finitude and contingency that is released by the question of historicity leads to the insight that the world that we inhabit is a world of unfreedom. But it also leads to the insight – and this is the paradox – that the world of unfreedom could become something else: it could become a world where freedom would be realized; and that is the great romantic dream of the young English and German philosophers and poets of the end of the eighteenth century, beginning of the nineteenth century, associated with Romanticism. The activity of critique defined by this insight into historicity is linked to the question of human emancipation. Critique and emancipation are two ends of the same piece of string, and the ever-flexible twine of that string, that is capable of producing new forms of oppression; as Hegel realized more powerfully than anybody else, the twine of that string is human freedom.

So, philosophy in the Continental tradition is inseparable from the relation to its tradition, its insight into history and historicity. But this isn't a conservative idea of tradition; it is what I would call a radical experience of tradition. Philosophy as I understand it is this activity that is defined through and through by the experience of historicity. But this isn't a conservative understanding of history, such as we would find in the classical political conservatism of Edmund Burke. Rather, it's an appeal to tradition, which is not at all traditional. What this radical idea of tradition is trying to recover is something missing, forgotten or repressed in contemporary life. What I want to show is the link between historicity, tradition and the possibility of transformation. So to summarize: tradition can be said to have two senses. We can talk about a tradition as something inherited or handed down without questioning or critical interrogation – this is a conservative idea of tradition – an acceptance of *doxa*, of common sense. Common sense as a guide in political and social life, what people like John Gray sometimes call political realism. And secondly, tradition can be something made or produced through a critical or deconstructive engagement with that first sense of tradition, an appeal to tradition that is in no way traditional, which is a phrase that Derrida uses in *Violence and Metaphysics*.

CC: *So it is this second sense of tradition that you want to defend, a tradition that does not attempt to forget and conceal its contingent origins?*

SC: Yes. For the later Husserl of the *Crisis of the European Sciences*, these two senses of tradition correspond to the distinction between a sedimented and a reactivated experience of tradition. And it helps to think of sedimentation in geological terms, as a process of settling or consolidation. For Husserl, sedimentation consists in the forgetfulness of the origin of a state of affairs, and the famous example here is the example of geometry, which appears in a text from 1936, called the *Origin of Geometry* – which was the subject of Derrida's first book – a translation of that text and then a long commentary on it. So I have also got Derrida in mind here –

very much so. Husserl's central argument, very simply stated, is that if one forgets the origin of geometry then one forgets the historical nature of disciplines like geometry. But why is this important? It's important because geometry expresses in its most pure form what Husserl calls the theoretical attitude, and the theoretical attitude is the stance that natural sciences take toward their objects. Husserl's point is that to reactivate the origin of geometry is to recall the way in which the theoretical attitude of the sciences belongs to a specific social and historical context, what Husserl famously calls the lifeworld, the *Lebenswelt*. Husserl's critical and polemical point – which is very important to me, and I tried to develop this in a critique of scientism in some work that I've done – is that the activity of science has, since Galileo, resulted in what he calls a mathematization of nature – a mathematization that overlooks the necessary dependence of science upon the practices of the lifeworld. And this is the situation that Husserl calls *crisis*.

CC: *So crisis here is when scientific knowledge, or scientism, becomes sedimented and ultimately covers over the contingency of science.*

SC: Yes, you can say that crisis occurs when the theoretical attitude of the sciences come to define the way in which all entities are viewed. This is the naturalistic worldview that is endemic to much professional philosophy, and is maybe the most widely shared *doxa* in Western culture; namely, that all entities should be explained by natural science or by natural scientific method, whether that is Darwinian, neuroscientific or whatever. The point of talking about Husserl here is that what we see in Husserl is the way in which an insight into historicity opens the space for a radical experience of tradition, and a critique of society as a society in crisis, which encloses an ethical demand that things should be otherwise organized. What you see in Husserl is the link between historicity, a radical experience of tradition and the idea that the society could be otherwise organized. And the condition of possibility for that is the generation of crisis.

CC: *And the philosopher's task is to generate a moment of crisis?*

SC: You could say that the responsibility of the philosopher is the production of genealogies which produce crisis. The worst situation for the philosopher is a situation where crisis is not recognized, where people would say 'crisis, what crisis?'. In a world where crisis is not recognized, I would argue, human beings sink to the level of happy cattle, a sort of bovine contentment that is systematically confused with happiness (but maybe that's a little mean to cows). The responsibility of the philosopher is the production of crisis.

CC: *And this is also the concern for Heidegger, that we have fallen into forgetfulness of Being.*

SC: Yes, things are not so different with the early Heidegger. For me, the question of finitude arose in relation to Heidegger's work, and the question of death. Heidegger's key concept here is the concept of what he calls destruction (*Destruktion*) or what he calls in his later work *Abbau*, dismantling or, literally, unbuilding. Destruction is the destruction of the history of ontology, Heidegger says. The history of ontology is not a way of destroying the past but of seeking the positive tendencies of that tradition, of working against what Heidegger labels in a nice phrase its 'baleful prejudices'. So we get destruction – and it is this word that Derrida translates as deconstruction in the mid-1960s; he was trying to find a French equivalent, which means that deconstruction is a genealogical operation – and this is a key insight. Destruction is the production of a tradition, a radical tradition, as something made and fashioned through a process of what Heidegger calls repetition or retrieval, *Wiederholung*. The thought here is that a genuine relation to tradition is achieved through an act of creative repetition, where I bring back – like with the example of Husserl – the original meaning of a state of affairs through an act of critical, historical, genealogical reflection. Now, Heidegger's central example – which is the one thought that stretches throughout his work – is the way in which the meaning of Being has been covered over in the tradition of Western metaphysics, since the time of the ancient Greeks, specifically since Aristotle's *Metaphysics*. So, we see the way in which the Husserlian insight into the origin of geometry takes on a different form in Heidegger. What Heidegger is trying to retrieve is an experience of Being, of that which *is*, which has been covered over. And that covering over for Heidegger is the experience of the West. It is what he calls, in a late text, the abandonment of Being.

The point here is that one has to destroy the received and banal sense of the past in order to experience the hidden and surprising power of history. And the power of history for Heidegger is the power of what he calls 'beginning'. Heidegger's thought is an attempt to think this idea of beginning; again, it's a controversial concept. In the period of *Being and Time*, in the late 1920s, Heidegger articulates the difference between a sedimented and a reactivated tradition – or a received and destroyed tradition – in terms of the distinction between what he calls tradition (*Tradition*) and heritage (*Überlieferung*). The idea of *Überlieferung* is very interesting. He's playing on the idea of *überliefern*, which means that something is disclosed and handed over to us. What Heidegger is trying to unleash through his meditation is the hidden potential of history. It's important to emphasize here that the target of Husserl's and Heidegger's reflections on tradition is not the past. They are not engaged in some antiquarian project, or some philological project. Their enquiry into tradition is aimed at the present, and this is also true of, say, Hegel's reflection on Spirit, which for him is motivated by the question of freedom; or Nietzsche's genealogy of nihilism, which for him is motivated by the question of life, the affirmation of life. The insight into historicity in the Continental tradition is not about getting the past right; it's a critique of the present, and the production of crisis in relation to the present.

Death

CARL CEDERSTRÖM: *To continue the previous discussion of Heidegger, to whom death and finitude are central themes, you write in your book* Very Little . . . Almost Nothing *that, to Heidegger, death is the possibility of impossibility. You then move on to criticize this notion through the work of Levinas and Blanchot, who claim the opposite: that death is the impossibility of possibility. Could you describe what the significance of death is in the work of Heidegger, and why you ultimately turn against it?*

SIMON CRITCHLEY: Let me begin by saying that death is a non-issue. One dies, big deal; everybody dies. In many ways, there is a powerful tradition of philosophical meditation on death that you find in Epicurus, Lucretius and Spinoza. Spinoza in the *Ethics* writes that the free man thinks of nothing less than death: death is a fact, which is of no particular importance. For me the key insight is the insight into finitude; finitude is not an issue of the fact that one dies at the end of one's life, but finitude is that moving limit of my life, which defines it and circumscribes it. In Heidegger, being-towards-death has four characteristics: it is certain; it is indeterminate; it is, he says, not to be outstripped; and it is non-relational. Let me explain those and you'll see where this is going. Death is certain: we're all going to die, big deal – it's a banal point. Death is indeterminate: we don't know when we're going to die, but we are going to die. Thirdly, death is not to be outstripped, which means that death is pretty important. But it's the fourth criterion – non-relationality – that is the key one.

And this is where the question of finitude becomes prob-
lematic. Heidegger asks, in the first chapter of Division Two
of *Being and Time*: can I understand the meaning of death
through the death of others? And the answer is no. The death
of others is the death of *others*; it's not my death. If I insist that
death is about the death of others, and not my own death,
I'm fundamentally missing the point. For Heidegger, nothing
can substitute for my relationship to my death. So death is not
relational; it's not about a relational experience to the other's
death; it's about *my* relationship to *my* death.

To understand that argument we have to understand the
first concept that Heidegger introduces in *Being and Time*'s
existential analytic, which is the concept of what he calls
'mineness' – *Jemeinigkeit*. The human being for Heidegger,
Dasein, is characterized by mineness. I am the sort of being for
whom being is the question, he says; the question of being is
fundamentally mine. And that concept then gets fed through
into his discussion of death, that the fundamental experience
of death is my relationship to my death. And then he says
– and this is the famous formulation – 'Death is the possibility of impossibility.' To have an inauthentic relationship to
death is to live through a relationship to others' deaths, or
just to not think about death; he says this is what animals do.
Animals just perish, they don't die. The only beings that die
truly are those beings that have a 'consciousness' of death or
an ability to reflect on it; that is, human beings. I think that's
another huge mistake in Heidegger. I think it's entirely possible, and probable, maybe even certain, that some animals
have an awareness of death: dolphins, elephants, maybe even
cats and dogs. No one can substitute for my death – death is
the possibility of impossibility. To have an authentic relationship to death is for *me* to seize hold of *my* relationship to *my*
death, and my death is that moment of impossibility. The
paradoxical formulation, possibility of impossibility, is that
Dasein is that being which is defined by possibility, that being

who can do things in the world, and the limit of that possibility is death. To be authentic, for Heidegger, is to internalize that limit of death, make it your own, and thereby act in the world. This is the condition of possibility for authenticity for Heidegger. To be authentic is to have internalized that finitude and to master it. We can master it, perhaps only for a moment, but we *can* master it.

CC: *And it is this idea of mastery and potency that you want to challenge in your work?*

SC: Yes, my reflections on death in *Very Little . . . Almost Nothing* begin from the contestation of that viewpoint, the Heideggerian viewpoint of mastery. The two thinkers who I've used to mobilize a critique of Heidegger are Levinas and Blanchot. The relation between Levinas and Blanchot is one of the most fascinating and puzzling in the history of twentieth-century thought because it's unclear what thought belongs to whom and concepts and themes sort of shuttled back and forth, like ping-pong, between them. But you find this phrase in both Blanchot and Levinas that *death is the impossibility of possibility*. The thought here, against Heidegger, is that it's *not* the case that death is that thing which can be internalized as the condition of possibility for authenticity. Rather, the human being is essentially defined by the *inability* to be. My fundamental experience is not an experience of non-relationality, but an experience of relationality.

Let me make that argument in relation to Levinas. Levinas only speaks about Heidegger publicly on two occasions in his life, once in 1940 and once again in 1987. And this is an extraordinary fact. Before he became popular in the 1980s, Levinas was known primarily as a scholar of Husserl and Heidegger. For him, the point of critical articulation in Heidegger's *Being and Time* is this question of death. Where Heidegger says that to die for another would be to sacrifice myself – or if I believe that another can substitute for my death – I'm missing the point. Levinas just inverts that. He says: Heidegger is exactly wrong; actually, my relationship to death does not come into the world through my relationship to my death, but through my relationship to the other's death. It is through the other's death – my bereavement, grief, mourning – that finitude gets a grip. *Very Little . . . Almost Nothing* was motivated by the death of my father and what I was trying to puzzle through in my grief was this issue: to think about the way in which death comes into the world through the other's death, and the way in which death is an impossibility. It's something over which I have no mastery: the other dies, I am bereaved, and I'm in a subjective position of radical impossibility. I cannot will the other's death away; that mourning, as it were, structures me. You find exactly the same structure of argument in Derrida's meditations on death, of which the most beautiful text for me is the meditations on Paul de Man, *Mémoires for Paul de Man*, where Derrida focuses on the theme of impossible mourning. To put it into a slogan: authentic *Dasein* in Heidegger is incapable of mourning. For Levinas, and for Derrida, the human being is essentially defined by an experience of impossible mourning, which means that one's subjectivity can never achieve mastery or authenticity, but is always already divided, broken up, by an experience of mourning.

CC: *Mourning is also closely associated with psychoanalysis and the work of Freud. What is the significance of Freud's work in relation to your thoughts about death?*

SC: Freud is essential for the way I think about death and the mourning that arises in relation to the other's death. In his essay, *Mourning and Melancholia*, from 1915, Freud says that normal mourning is that activity where the beloved other is dead: my world is shattered, it no longer has meaning and I suffer. Then Freud makes what sounds like a callous remark – but it's profound, though maybe not easy to achieve. He says that in normal mourning I can eventually overcome my grief of the other, I can internalize the other – again, this is in Freud's very simplistic subject-object language – the other as external factor disappears. The fucker is dead, I can internalize that, and if I internalize that successfully I can get over it. He says in *Mourning and Melancholia* that 'by taking flight into the ego, love escapes extinction' – it's an amazing line. So love survives by internalizing itself. It ceased to be an object of love; love has become an internal memory. And if I can overcome my grief, I can love again, love someone else again. Where that doesn't happen is in the experience of what we might call 'abnormal mourning', or melancholia. In abnormal mourning I just don't get over the other's death; that other's death takes flight into the ego – sure – but it takes flight in a way that haunts and divides that ego in a way that leaves it troubled. This is the melancholic ego. In many ways, what I'm arguing for is a melancholic idea of finitude: death comes into the world through the death of others, and it's something we never get over. It's something which simply lives in us, and it lives in us as something we cannot be adequate to; and those ghosts haunt us. For me, this is the fundamental experience of the strand of modernist literature which I love.

CC: *Which perhaps brings us to your interest in Ibsen? You say in that essay* ['Noises Off – On Ibsen'] – *and I think this neatly captures the uncanny experience of being haunted – that what one inherits are ghosts and that these ghosts constitute an existential debt that we can never make up.*

SC: Well, I gave this talk on Ibsen, which appeared in an obscure Norwegian journal, because I'm not happy with it. I called it 'Noises Off', which is the theatrical expression for unwanted off-stage sounds. My claim, or my theme, is that what defines the awful, claustrophobic, domestic space of Ibsen's dramas – this Norwegian hell in bourgeois houses – is noise; and I tried to track the theme of noise in all of Ibsen's dramas. And in a great many of his dramas you can hear noise: the noise of rainfall in *Ghosts*; the noises in *Little Eyolf*: the noise of rats, scratching under the floor. This is always an uncanny, unsettling experience. And these are the ghosts who won't let us go: they won't let us sleep, they won't let us rest. This is the experience of what Levinas calls the *il y a*, that ever-present background hum of being, which for me is just a breathtakingly wonderful concept. Levinas begins from a thought experiment. He says there are certain thinkers who think the fundamental experience is the experience of being, like Heidegger for example; and that experience of being is an experience of clearing or lighting, *die Lichtung des Seins*, as Heidegger calls it. Levinas inverts this by saying: think about the case when the experience of being is not an experience of clearing, lighting, illumination and wonder, but an experience of darkness, horror and this sort of claustrophobic proximity to something that can't be internalized. This is the experience of the night. He's thinking of childhood experiences but also experiences that extend way beyond childhood, where you lay awake at night. In that experience of the dark, there is a reversal of intentionality. It's no longer the ego that regards objects in the world and makes epistemic claims about them – or in Husserl's sense that I could manipulate those things for my use, like Heidegger with his hammer. Instead, it is an experience when things turn and look at me, when, as Paul Klee says 'things look at me', '*les choses me regardent*'. This is the reversal of intentionality in the experience of the night. There's an oppressive experience of the night in insomnia, which is the experience of the *il y a*, and, again, that's an experience of impossibility. I can't make myself sleep. In insomnia there's that experience of a fundamental openness of the human being to something that will not let it rest, and this for Levinas is a fundamental experience.

CC: *But this experience is also biographical in the sense that you are suffering from tinnitus.*

SC: Yes, and I think there's maybe something a little perverse here. *Very Little . . . Almost Nothing* is a meditation on my father's death. But I couldn't do that directly, because what was I going to say except that that I loved him and I still miss him? It's banal. So I did that indirectly through a series of philosophical or conceptual structures, hundreds of pages. The other thing is my relation to tinnitus. I've been obsessed, in a whole number of authors, with what I call the tinnitus of existence, this background noise which seems to frame human life and drain it of all meaning: and that's because I've suffered from tinnitus for 25 years. As I said earlier, I'm trying to find some way of thinking about that in my work. Ibsen for me is about this tinnitus of existence, this overwhelming hum. You can block it out, with chatter or television. So there's definitely a strong link between, as it were, conceptuality and biography.

CC: *To go back to the theme of sound or even more so, to the concept of the* il y a: *in your work on* Phaedra *you say that existence for her is without exit; that her life is impossible.*

SC: *Phaedra* is a drama that I read when I was about 22 and it completely blew me away. I saw a production of it in London by the Wooster group, a New York theater group. But when I saw it, it was called 'To you, The Birdie!', and it was an adaptation of Racine's *Phaedra* – where the world of the French court, projected back on the Greek aristocratic world, became a badminton court, and shuttlecocks were sent back and forth throughout the play. That was, as it were, the unreal world of everyday life and it was against that that Phaedra defined herself. So Phaedra is defined by desire, and it is the desire for sex with her stepson. She wants to fuck him. And Phaedra's desire isn't just any desire – and here we come back to ghosts – because it's the desire of her mother. Her mother, Pasiphaë, was fucked by the Minotaur, in the labyrinth, in Crete, and in order to be fucked by the great bull – because he wouldn't fuck just anyone – she had Daedalus construct an artificial wooden cow. She then crouched inside the wooden cow and the bull approached her and penetrated her. So her mother engaged in illicit love with a bull, and it's that maternal desire that flows through Phaedra's veins: but she doesn't consummate the desire with her stepson. She wants to die. This is where things get interesting – and this goes back to the question of impossibility. If she kills herself, which she does in the drama – she dies in the drama – then where does she go? She goes down to Hades, and in Hades her father, King Minos, is the judge. So what's going to happen when his daughter shows up in Hades, in front of her father? This is the paternal desire: 'Why are you here my daughter?' And she responds, 'Because I was also fuelled by the same desire as your wife Pasiphaë when she wanted to be fucked by the bull.' Life on earth is impossible for Phaedra, because she lives with a desire that she cannot control; and death is impossible, because when she dies she'll go to Hades and there she will be judged by her father. She can't die, and she can't live. So Phaedra is defined by this experience of impossibility.

CC: *She's possessed by that which she cannot escape, you write in your text on Phaedra, and you then link this to originary inauthenticity and sin. Could you develop that argument?*

SC: Original sin is the theological expression of an ontological defectiveness of the human being, that there's something essentially flawed about what it means to be human. You find this in Paul, Augustine, Luther and others. Original sin is the idea that we're essentially constituted by a lack at the heart of our being, a lack that we cannot make up and whose origin goes back to our origin – namely the story of the fall – and can only be redeemed through faith in Christ. What you find in Racine are these examples from the pagan world, the Greek world, through which he explores that dimension of original sin – namely, that the human being is marked by a defectiveness, a facticity that I cannot make up or make good.

CC: *And this is the experience of melancholia?*

SC: Melancholia is a relationship to an unknown loss. The melancholic ego seems to be defined by an open wound that won't heal – those are Freud's words – and that wound is the wound of sin, in my view. And this is something I come back to repeatedly in my work, in a way that I neither really understand, nor am able to control. It's there in the mystical anarchism material in the new book, *The Faith of the Faithless*.

CC: *Also, it's there in much of your writing on Beckett. What I find appealing about Beckett's world – and this is something that comes through in your analyses, I think – is that there's no escape. The subject finds itself in a world defined by impossibility. It's almost as if the world itself is suffering from this wound that won't heal?*

SC: Absolutely. It's the sin of the world. The world in Becket is the world that has been devastated. By what? We're never told. Even people as clever as Adorno say that perhaps it has something to do with the Holocaust, or perhaps to do with the threat of nuclear war. But Beckett is far too clever to identify the cause. We live in a world of sin, a world defined by a radical lack of meaning in which human beings circulate: they move; they go to-and-fro, back-and-forth. The great paradigm for this is *Waiting for Godot*, which is in two acts, and it's a play where nothing happens twice: like *Groundhog Day* or growing up in Hertfordshire. Nothing happens in the first act, and then nothing happens again. And the second act is a repetition of the first act, almost exactly, though with some key differences. It's a situation where nothing happens and there's not even the possibility of memory. The most poignant moment – oh, there's so many poignant moments in *Godot*! – but the one I'm thinking of now is when the boy comes on, at the end of both acts, and says that Godot is not coming today. They ask the boy: 'Does Mr Godot treat you well? does he beat you?' 'No, he beats my brother, sir.' And this goes back and forth. But the key thing is that Vladimir says: 'But tell Mr Godot that you saw us. You'll tell him that you saw us?' And in the second act it becomes even more acute: 'Tell him that you saw us. You did see us, didn't you?' 'Yes sir', the boy says and he then leaves. And the play ends with the phrase 'Let's go', and nothing happens, nobody moves. What you have in Beckett is this sin of the world, where nothing happens, and there's just this repetitive loop of absence.

CC: *How about the possibility of death in Beckett?*

SC: This is true of Beckett's characters from the Trilogy all the way through to these late texts like *Company* – the voice in *Company* is alone at night, propped up in a bed, 'there comes a voice' – there's always a voice coming from elsewhere. *Molloy* begins with Molloy in his mother's bed, but what is he doing in his mother's bed? How did he get there? In an ambulance? Perhaps. In a vehicle of some sort? 'It is I that live here now.' His mother is dead, but that's not even clear. But he lives in his mother's room and this is something which touches on Beckett's own experience. Beckett was in psychoanalysis with Wilfrid Bion when the latter was a candidate in London, just beginning his career. I think the analysis lasts the entirety of 1935 and 1936, and apparently it helped. But Beckett was in analysis arguably because of what he called his mother's 'savage loving' and his mother paid for his psychoanalysis. And this was after Beckett's father had just died. It is perhaps only after one's father dies that one realizes the extent of one's relationship to one's mother, I think, and her savage loving. The characters in Beckett are in this world of ghosts, like Ibsen, but without the possibility of there being any tragic *dénouement*, as there is in Ibsen. At least the characters in Ibsen can kill themselves; at least Hedda Gabler can get her father's pistol and blow her brains out, pregnant as she is at the time; extraordinary scene. The characters in Beckett couldn't do that. There's still the possibility of tragedy in Ibsen, whereas in Beckett it's what he calls tragicomedy, which means that if you did manage to get a gun, there would be no bullets in it. Or, when Vladimir and Estragon are trying to hang themselves in *Godot*, they cannot find a tree, or a rope, or whatever.

CC: *You have said, in another context, that impotence could be your badge of honour. What's the significance of impotence?*

SC: Beckett's characters are marked by a fundamental impotence. If what defines *Dasein*, the human being in Heidegger, is potentiality for Being, then *Dasein* is the being that *can*; the being that is potent. What I find in my gallery of moribunds, my cast of heroes – Levinas, Blanchot, Beckett and the rest – are that they are fundamentally subjects that *can't*, subjects that are defined by impotence, and that impotence is an impotence in relationship to the death of others – the death of the mother or father – but also in relationship to their own deaths. If we turn to *Malone Dies*, the key thing about that book is the title, which just means that Malone dies or is dying *(meurt)*. Beckett keeps giving up the story, keeps being unable to tell the story. It's someone in bed, atrophied, powerless, fundamentally impotent, narrating his own dying. And what's being narrated in that dying is the impossibility of death, the impossibility of death being a condition of possibility for authenticity. This led me in *Very Little . . . Almost Nothing* to make a distinction, which I borrow from Blanchot, between death (*la mort*) and dying (*le mourir*). For me the fundamental experience of finitude is the experience of an impotence in relationship to the fact of one's dying. Now, that sounds bleak on one level, but for me, and we will come to this in a later discussion, that's the condition for humour; but it's also the condition for something like courage. Something I learnt from Badiou's book on Beckett is that what defines Beckett's work is an ethics of courage; but that ethics of courage is measured against an acceptance of fundamental impotence – there's a line in Molloy: 'Where did I get this access of vigour? From my weakness perhaps.' Beckett says things like: 'There is rapture, or there should be, in the motion crutches give.' We go from Molloy on his bicycle, to Molloy unable to ride his bicycle, to Malone in bed dying, unable to get up, to the unnamable, Mahood, who is stuck like a sheaf of flowers in a glass pot, in the shambles areas of a city – it might be Dublin but it might not – but it's in the vicinity of the slaughter house. This character Mahood is looking at a horse's ass and feels some flicker of sexual excitement and he says: 'The tumefaction of the penis! The penis, well now . . . What a pity I have no arms.' This essential recognition of impotence of the human being is the condition of possibility for courage and action. To flip it the other way around, the obsession with authenticity and potency is what is genuinely horrific.

CC: *Another thing that I find fascinating about the characters in Beckett's trilogy is that they keep on writing, obsessionally. Malone has to continue writing; writing his own death.*

SC: One wants to write one's death but all that one can write is one's dying. 'As I lay dying', as Faulkner puts it. Dying is that thing that one tries to narrate but which cannot be narrated – it's the limit of narration. To summarize this: for me, if philosophy is the activity of critique defined by historicity, and if the basis for that is the recognition of finitude, then finitude can go in many directions, and we have named two. On the one hand, we have finitude as what Heidegger calls being-towards-death, which is the condition of possibility for authenticity, potency and mastery, and which leads to an idea of death as non-relational. On the other hand we have the idea of an essentially relational account of finitude: where finitude is not an expression of potency or strength, but an expression of impotence and weakness; and where finitude is marked by the ghosts of those that one loves or hates – those ghosts that won't let you go. And it's a finitude which is fundamentally defined by the inability to actually relate to the fact of oneself; a finitude that cannot be mastered.

CC: *You write in* Very Little . . . Almost Nothing *that suicide is impossible. Could you explain that?*

SC: My view of suicide is Freudian and is linked to the experience of melancholia that I was talking about before. If mourning is the experience of loss in relation to the loved object, as Freud puts it in a rather heartless way, then melancholia is a relationship to an unknown loss, a loss that is essentially a loss in relation to a wound that the ego has inflicted. The melancholic experiences himself or herself in terms of this division between themselves and some aspect of themselves that has been lost. So melancholia is fundamentally characterized by this experience of division. And this can be exemplified in a number of phenomena. Freud says that when we listen to the melancholic talk about himself or herself it's as if they're talking about another person. These things seem to be undergone by somebody else – it's as if I'm talking about a third or second person out there. It can be exemplified in, say, the phenomenon of anorexia, where the anorexic experiences themselves in relationship to the image they have of themselves in the mirror: their body is still too fat and needs to be sufficiently starved in order to become beautiful. Melancholia is this division between the self and a hated other, the hated other that one is, somehow externalized and objectified. I think that's how I'd approach suicide. What one is killing, when killing oneself, is not oneself – it's the hated other that one has become: I want to kill that disgusting piece of shit that doesn't deserve to live; it's *that* creature that has to die. To that extent, suicide is impossible. Suicide is homicide; it's murder. It's murder of that hated other that I am.

CC: *Much of what you have said so far points to the impossibility of death. However, in your interpretation of Terrence Malick's film,* The Thin Red Line, *you speak about a calm that Witt experiences at the moment of his death. This almost seems like the romantic idea of death, where death is suddenly possible.*

SC: So, the hero of *The Thin Red Line* is this character Witt. And we meet him for the first time on the beach meditating about his mother's death, imagining that he could meet death with the same calm that his mother seemed to meet it. We then get this romantic flashback: it's somewhere in the Midwest; he's touching his mother's hand; then the hand is pulled away and she's gone. That's the fantasy of the authentic death. And Witt, according to Malick, fulfils that fantasy: approaching death with calm – this is Epicurus, Lucretius, Spinoza. Interestingly, when I was looking at the sources – and he's very faithful to Jim Jones's novel *The Thin Red Line* – he inserts the word 'calm' into that passage, it's not there in the novel. It might or might not be an allusion to Heidegger, where Heidegger talks about anxiety as an anxiety towards death as an experience of calm, or peace: the German is *Ruhe*. This is a Romantic idea of death. For Heidegger, if human beings are authentic they're heading towards death; if they're inauthentic they experience demise, which means that we just pass out of existence. But only animals and plants perish, and that just seems to be ridiculous. Human beings perish all the time, can perish, and there are examples like in Kafka's *Trial* where one dies like a dog. Human beings die in all sorts of ways, in a permanent vegetative state, or whatever.

CC: *Sure. Death – like perversity – is polymorphous. I absolutely agree with that. Now, another thing that I want to discuss with you is the meaning of death in our contemporary society. You write in* The Book of Dead Philosophers *that death is everywhere. Yet we are suspiciously reluctant to speak about it, as if it is our last great taboo. Could you elaborate on that claim?*

SC: We believe ourselves to be anti-Victorians in the sense that Victorians had a problem with sex but an elaborate culture of death: a moralization and memorialization of death; a ritualization and monumentalization of death in Victorian graveyard architecture, and all the rest. We have no problem with sex: sex is allegedly something we have a right to, the right to orgasm whenever and with whomever we like, or so we fantasize. But death is something we are unable to face up to. Of course this is a ridiculous caricature: we have as many problems with sex as the Victorians, and maybe we're in a worse situation because we have developed a discourse around sexuality based on the belief that personal fulfilment, or personal authenticity, is bound up with the expression of sexuality. But it is undeniably the case that we flee the fact of death. Death has become taboo. Our relation to death is one of evasion or escape; we escape it through denial of death, or fleeing into forgetfulness, living in what

Sartre called a counterfeit immortality – believing this will go on forever – or we escape the fact of death through forms of belief in the afterlife, which has taken on new variants. It's no longer a belief in the immortality of the soul, which in many ways is a much more plausible view, but people believe in the immortality of the body at some level, which can continue to live through techniques of cryonic freezing; or people believe in some sort of Buddhistic or quasi-Buddhistic idea of death, not as an end, but as a continuation: death as a state of growth. People have a completely materialistic understanding of human life, and somehow believe that their material substance is going to continue in some new form after their demise. We have an incredibly confused relationship to our mortality.

CC: *So perhaps one could say that the motivation for writing this book was to reassert, and think anew, the age-old motto of the philosophical death, where the highest achievement was to die well?*

SC: Yes. The reason why I wrote *The Book of Dead Philosophers* was in order to confront that question and to defend the idea and the ideal of the philosophical death. The heroes in this story are many, but the main hero is Montaigne. Montaigne's view, which is his return to Ciceronian and Socratic wisdom, is that to philosophize is to learn how to die. There's this extraordinary line that I'd like to quote from Montaigne where he says: 'He who has learnt how to die has unlearnt how to be a slave.' The idea is that slavery consists in the slavery to the fear of death, and it's that fear of death that keeps us constantly on the gasp, constantly running, escaping, or evading. If slavery consists in slavery to the fear of death, then the idea of the philosophical death is to no longer be a slave. You find this line of thought in Epicurus in the most powerful way, that for him the four-part-cure, *tetrapharmakos*, at the core of Epicurean wisdom is as follows: 'Do not fear God, do not fear death; what is good is easy to get, and what is painful is easy to endure.' The gods somehow exist for Epicurus, but in a distant way: they exist in the interstices of the cosmos, and they are of no importance. Pleasure is something that should be cultivated, but pleasure should be minimized to be cultivated; one should limit one's pleasures. For Epicurus, that meant a barley cake and a glass of water, and on occasion some potted cheese, or whatever. So by minimizing one's pleasures, the withdrawal of those pleasures could also be minimized – so by limiting pleasure, one limits pain. Therefore, on this view, what should be avoided are extreme pleasures, because they would lead to extreme pains when they're absent. Epicurus thought that drunkenness or intoxication, or sexual pleasure in particular, were extreme pleasures that should be avoided. It was a very peculiar hedonism of minimal pleasures, bound up with an asceticism in relation to sexual life. If this were properly cultivated, it would lead to the fourth part of the cure, which is not fearing death. What one has to take from the Epicurean cure, the *pharmakos*, is the the removal of longing for immortality. It is the longing for immortality that makes us suffer. For Epicurus – and you find this expressed in a more articulate way in Lucretius' *On the Nature of the Universe* – since we have no anxiety about the time before our birth, we should have no anxiety about the time after our death. This is based on the argument for equivalence, namely the equivalence of the time after our death and before our birth. On the Epicurean view, you overcome the fear of death by making death nothing. And that nothing isn't just a passage to some transcendent beyond, as it is in Socrates or Plato, where you find these peculiar arguments for immortality, but a nothing that insists on a completely materialist understanding of nature. I find this argument compelling in Epicurus; namely, that a completely materialist understanding of nature can induce an experience of calm, of tranquillity, or what the Epicurean calls *ataraxia*, in relationship to the conduct of one's life. You find this idea picked up in Spinoza, that the free man thinks of nothing less than death, that once you learnt to see things from the standpoint of eternity, you realize that death is nothing and you can live a free life insofar as you moderate your affects. Extreme passions should be avoided. Affects, Spinoza says, have to be moderated so they don't become extreme passions.

CC: *There's something really seductive about this thought. At the same time it seems to flirt with another kind of fantasy, the fantasy of being able to look upon ourselves from a non-human perspective. In a way, we are not just incapable of introspection; we are also incapable of seeing ourselves from an external and material point of view.*

SC: Yes. The problem with the Spinozist idea is that life isn't like that. To look at things from the standpoint of eternity is appealing, but it misses something essential about what it means to be human. You're absolutely right. There's a line in Wittgenstein where I think he's picking up on this line of enquiry, almost unconsciously, that the 'eternal life is given to those who live in the present'; insofar as one can live in the present, one can look at things under the aspect of eternity, and remove the fear of death. The problem is that the argument for equivalence is phenomenologically implausible. This is something that Thomas Nagel pointed out in his classic article on death: existence has a projective, forward-looking character. The future that is coming to us and even that which follows my death is of enormous concern, but the past that existed before our birth is of no concern. We're living in a 'now' that is constantly opening onto the future, and the anticipation of that is what structures human life. Is it possible to live under the aspect of eternity? Maybe for a moment; maybe in certain experiences. But the fact of anxiety kicks back in.

CC: *How does this touch on the question of the fear of death?*

SC: *The Book of Dead Philosophers* has this idea of death as the last taboo, as you mentioned. The history of philosophy is a history of deaths, which can be instructive as a series of moments; for instance, it can remind a culture that denies death of the reality of death, and that's interesting. Up to a certain point I want to defend the idea of the philosophical death. The problem with it – and this is something that I broach in the book, but don't really do justice to – is that there is something finally selfish and self-satisfied and obsessional about the philosopher's way of dying. I think you see this most obviously in the person of Socrates in the *Phaedo*. In my reading of that dialogue, he produces arguments for the immortality of the soul, which are pretty implausible. I don't think that Socrates believes his arguments for the immortality of the soul for a minute. I think that he wants to die in his own way, in a manner of his choosing, at a time of his choosing. And that's why, for example, he asks the fatal draft of poison to be mixed rather early in the evening. His disciples say 'no, it's perfectly okay to go right through the night; you can take the poison much later on', and Socrates replies, 'No, I want to do it now; get it over with.' I see Socrates also as an Epicurean. I don't think he believes in the immortality of the soul at all. He's just throwing out these stories to assuage his disciples and make them feel better, whereas he just wants to die.

CC: *Again, this points to a rather detached and seemingly rational response to the question of death – a response that only briefly touches upon the more indigestible aspects of the experience of death, such as grief, mourning and guilt. These aspects weren't really that central to Greek thought, were they?*

SC: Well, obviously the Greeks mourned, and had elaborate death rituals for regulating affect within socially acceptable limits (grieving too much was a characteristic of barbarians, for the ancient Greeks). But I think the whole question of death takes on a different intensity in Christianity. Here, the key figure is St Augustine, but also, to go back a bit, St Paul. We talked before about original sin as the basic ontological defectiveness of the human being, which can only be addressed through the experience of faith and love. But with the fact of sin, what also came into the world is the fact of death. The experience of mortality, for Paul, is something I'm not in control of, something I cannot master. It's a fact about myself that is true; it is something which I've inherited from the ghosts of the past, and which I cannot master. In Augustine it takes on a different intensity. Augustine's *Confessions* is punctuated by three deaths: the death of his friend, the death of his mother and the death of his son. The death of his friend – and this is in *Book IV* of the *Confessions* when Augustine is still a pagan – grieves Augustine with a terrific intensity; he felt that his friend was part of his soul. In losing his friend he lost part of his soul. So for Augustine it was incredibly difficult, if not impossible, to carry on. But that's when he was a pagan. When he becomes a Christian his mother dies, Santa Monica. She's happy that Augustine has become a Christian and she betrays no fear of death because she knows that she's going to have an immortal life. When she's asked how she wants her body to be disposed of she says: 'I don't care; God will find me wherever I drop'. But when she dies, Augustine is thrown into this extraordinary experience of both feeling grief for his mother's death and knowing that he shouldn't feel grief, because he's a Christian and therefore going to be guaranteed immortal life. Augustine is divided over and against himself, between a grief that he feels and guilt for feeling that grief – it's an extraordinary moment. He wrestles with that and eventually overcomes it. The third death is the death of his son, Adeodatus, which is mentioned in half a line, in passing, where Augustine simply says that 'my son died; it was okay; we'd both been baptized as Christians in Milan the previous year, and he went to a better place'.

For reasons I have not fully understood, the experience of mourning and grief takes on a deeper intensity in Christianity, and this links back to what I was saying before about the philosophical death and then, before that, about the question of finitude. I think it's grief that gives us a fundamental experience of mortality. It's grief that, as I say in *The Book of Dead Philosophers*, unstitches our carefully tailored suit of the self. So, what we have in Socrates – and Socrates follows Epicurus – is a carefully tailored suit of the self that is trying to confront death with integrity. Grief undoes that; rips it asunder. The risk of the idea of the philosophical death is the risk of self-satisfaction, selfishness and obsessionality. What the experience of grief does is to blow that apart. This is where I want to criticize the idea of the philosophical death.

CC: *In* The Book of Dead Philosophers *you concentrate on a series of pairs that I find extremely fascinating. The relationship between Heidegger and Wittgenstein is one such pair. Heidegger would speak endlessly about the relationship between death and Being in his work, while avoiding dangerous situations in life (he was serving in a meteorological unit during the First World War). Wittgenstein, in contrast, did not see death as an event with any philosophical importance, while in his life, or at least in his life during the war, he would put himself into situations of extreme danger. Now, there's another of these pairs that I find particularly interesting with regard to the philosophical death, and that is the pair of Foucault and Derrida. You write that whereas Foucault faced death like a classical philosopher, Derrida couldn't. Could you elaborate on your position in relation to these two figures?*

SC: Foucault, in his last years, moves into the question of history of sexuality and moves back from being a historian of the early modern period into antiquity. Volumes II and III of *The History of Sexuality* are about many things, but they're essentially concerned with idea of the 'care of the self' as a practice of freedom. What is going on in Foucault is an attempt to retrieve the stoical relationship to death that you find in Seneca – Seneca was very much on Foucault's mind in the last years. Foucault, who is an early victim of AIDS – and it would appear from the evidence that he knew he had a fatal disease, though AIDS was only just being diagnosed at that time, in the early 1980s – dies the philosophical death; he dies the Senecan, stoical death. Derrida, by contrast, says in his last major interview, which is an amazing conversation with *Le Monde*: 'I remain uneducatable with respect to the wisdom of learning to die.' For Derrida, the idea that to philosophize is to learn how to die is repugnant. This explains, I think, why Derrida was so obsessed with the death of others: from the time of his essay on the death of Roland Barthes, which was in 1980, all the way through to shortly before his own death, when he's writing obituary after obituary about other people's deaths. What's motivating that is a sheer inability to become reconciled to the fact of one's death – a sheer terror of mortality. This goes back to themes of mourning, that those others that have died mark the self. A crowd of ghosts that circle the self. This gallery of moribunds whose portraits I stare at blankly divide me from myself. I guess now I find that Derridean approach to mortality perhaps more honest. There's something simply terrifying about the fact of death in a way that cannot be assuaged by the idea of the philosophical death. And furthermore, that idea of the philosophical death is perhaps finally a selfish male ideal that needs to be rethought. This is a realization I've come to in the past year or so. I was asked to give a talk in London last year on the topic of 'how to live'. I answered the question by talking about the philosophical death. To know how to live is to know how to die; and by internalizing death within oneself, one can overcome the fear of death. But if that how-to-live question is essentially selfish and obsessional, then there's a second question, which for me has become more pressing; which is the issue of how to love. What does love tell us about the nature of the self – and that's something that I've begun to think about in my recent work.

Love

CARL CEDERSTRÖM: *Let us continue with the remark you made in the last chapter: that the ideal of the philosophical death has appeared to you more and more as a selfish and obsessional ideal, and that you have now begun to consider love as an alternative response to the question of how to live. Indeed, much of your work has been motivated by the question of death. But until now, you have remained rather silent on the topic of love (though, in my mind, I think it latently runs through much of your work). So my first question is this: how would you place love in relation to death?*

SIMON CRITCHLEY: If to philosophize is to learn how to die, then this means that human existence is defined by the fact of finitude, and finitude has to be that limit – but the ever-moving limit, because we're moving through existence – in relation to which life is lived. The history of philosophy has been about, arguably, little more than that question. Philosophy is an art of dying – an art of dying well, *ars moriendi*, from Socrates to Heidegger. But shouldn't this obsession with death invite some suspicion? I've begun to think so in the last couple of years. Hannah Arendt, in *The Life of the Mind*, criticizes philosophers, male philosophers, for their persistent obsession with death to the exclusion of the question of birth. For her, the issue is about natality, on the one hand, and the question of love, on the other – her doctoral dissertation was on the question of love in Augustine. Is philosophy capable of thinking the question of love? On one level the obvious answer is: yes, sure – philosophy is the love of wisdom. So philosophy begins with a critique of the sophists; the sophists are those people who claim to know and offer to exchange knowledge for a fee. Philosophy begins with a critique of sophistry and its claims to knowledge. In place of the sophistical pretension to wisdom, philosophy offers a *love* of wisdom, a *philia*, an orientation of the soul towards the true, which is not the possession of the true. So philosophy begins with love in a non-erotic sense: a kind of friendship, usually between men, usually between an older man and a younger man, a little like our conversations, Carl! How reactionary we are!

CC: *Indeed. But you have never addressed the question of love directly.*

SC: For me, the question of love – and this is no doubt for biographical reasons – is elusive. For about 20 years or so I've been promising myself to write something about the *Song of Songs*, or the *Song of Solomon*, which strangely finds its way into the Bible. What's extraordinary in the *Song of Songs* is that we have an erotic love poem, which seems to have been written for nuptial celebrations, and which seems to have been stitched together from a whole range of different frag-ments. What's fascinating about this love poem is that it is a song, which is sung with different voices – in particular a male voice, and a female voice. What we have in the *Song of Songs* is a truly carnal experience of erotic love. For instance: your breasts are like two fawns, his loins are the smoothest ivory, your vulva a rounded crater – may it never lack punch! And so on. It's very saucy, particularly when read in a literal translation from the Hebrew. There are philosophers like Luce Irigaray who have claimed that what we find in the *Song of Songs* is the possibility of an ethics of sexual difference. To go back to Arendt's point: if philosophers have been overly concerned with the question of mortality, then there's also a sense in which this is a problem that male philosophers have had. And what Irigaray tries to show in the *Song of Songs* is that here we have an *active* female voice speaking to an *active* male voice, in celebration of a nuptial erotic encounter.

I stumbled back into that text about two and a half years ago, when I was teaching Levinas; but once again I ended up not writing on it, because the following thing happened. I began to look at how the *Song of Songs* had been received, particularly within Christianity. And what's striking is that the discourse of mysticism in the Middle Ages begins with a series of interpretations of the *Song of Songs*, in Bernard de Clairvaux, Meister Eckhart and elsewhere. And the carnal love of a man for his wife, and a wife for a husband, becomes a more spiritual love – the expression of God's love for Israel in Judaism and Christ's love for his church, and the church's love for Christ, in Christianity. So I then began to become fascinated with mystical interpretations of the *Song of Songs*, and then the mystical experience of love. What happened next is that I became particularly concerned with female mystics, and in particular one female mystic called Marguerite Porete, a Beguine who was burned at the stake in 1310 in Paris – a woman from a fairly noble or bourgeois family, who was propagating a doctrine of what she called refined love, *fine amor*, and this began to fascinate me. She was burned at the stake with great reluctance by the authorities, it appears, because she refused to recant her views in her book, which was called – and it's the most beautiful title – *The Mirror of Simple and Annihilated Souls and Those Who Remain in Longing and Desire of Love*. This text is written both in the style of the courtly romance love of the medieval period and also in the style of a dialogue where the model is Boethius' *Consolation of Philosophy*. But there's something really radical going on in Porete. What she describes at the core of this book are the seven stages of the soul's annihilation; and let me try and sketch those in thumbnail and try and pick out what I think is so compelling about this.

CC: *Please do.*

SC: For me, love is not, as Hegel says, a relationship of dependence between independent beings, which sounds like some sort of contractual relationship, like a marriage. Love isn't that. Love is something much more excessive and transgressive, and I think this is what you find in Porete. What she describes are the seven stages through which the soul can pass in order to bring about its own annihilation. And this means, in the first stage, that we have to follow the Ten Commandments and then, secondly, we have to follow the basic doctrines of Christianity. And then she says, thirdly and more dramatically, that one must hew and hack away at oneself in order to make a space that is large enough for love to enter. So love is the activity of a masochistic emptying of the self – the attempt to annihilate the self. The fourth stage of the annihilation of the soul is an experience of delight – drunken delight, intoxication with the divine. The fifth stage is an experience of dereliction and distance from God. But it's the sixth stage that is most interesting. While the seventh stage is already what happens after our death – we can't know much about that, we're simply joined with God in everlasting life – in the sixth stage she describes what's happened when the soul is annihilated. When the soul is annihilated, God – in whatever sense God has here – enters the self and the space where the soul was, and the annihilation of the soul is replaced by the infinite self-reflection of the divine. This is why she was burnt at the stake: because what she's describing in *The Mirror of Simple Annihilated Souls* is the annihilation of the soul as the condition of possibility for the union with the divine. Where the soul was, there God shall be, in some form. What is being envisaged by Porete is the possibility of a sinless, ecstatic union with the divine. This is heresy, because to achieve this state, nothing more is required than the cultivation of love in your soul. There is no need for the agency of the church and its moral strictures. This is why she was burned at the stake. Now, I'm not arguing that we should become God.

CC: *There's an interesting connection to psychoanalysis here. I'm thinking of Freud's puzzling remark,* Wo Es war, soll Ich werden, *(where the id was, there ego shall be), which seems to be an inverted form of what you're now describing, that 'where the soul was, there God shall be'.*

SC: Yes. What Porete is trying to describe is the transformation of the self through an act of love. And to link that to psychoanalysis, there's a fascinating moment in Lacan's *Seminar XX*, where he stumbles upon Beguine mysticism, medieval mysticism. And this is where he's trying to describe the experience of feminine enjoyment, or *jouissance*, and its relationship to love. And Lacan says (I quote): 'These mystical jaculations are neither idle chatter nor empty verbiage.' There's a fantastic book by Norman Cohn, *The Pursuit of the Millennium*, in which he identifies the famous heresy of the free spirit and the tradition of mystical anarchism as animating heresies in the Middle Ages. These lead through to contemporary forms of utopianism which he's very suspicious of, and he thinks that mystical discourse is a sort of veneer for sexual licence. And Lacan makes an extraordinary remark, as if he were replying to Cohn; he says: 'to reduce mysticism to the business of fucking is to miss the point entirely' – and I agree with that. If we go back to the *Song of Songs* – and this is what I'm writing about right now, so it's not properly formulated – what interests me in the experience of love is not the direct description of carnal desire but the spiritualization of desire in a form of *ascesis*, in a form of abstinence and discipline. Lacan says (and he's thinking not of Porete, whom he clearly didn't know, but of Hadewijch of Antwerp and Teresa of Avila, who's on the front cover of *Seminar XX*, in the ecstasy of Bernini's statue), 'I believe in the *jouissance* of woman insofar as it is an extra (*en plus*)'. And this is what's interesting: that female mystics are on the path of an experience of the *en plus*, an experience of transgression that exceeds the order of knowledge. What interests me with the question of love is that dimension of transgression, which Lacan elsewhere identifies with truth. This truth is not a propositional truth or an empirical truth, but some sort of ecstatic experience of truth.

It's that which really interests me – that there is something excessive in the experience of *jouissance*, in the experience of love, that is always more. Obviously, you can take this back to Lacan's interpretation of Antigone. Antigone as being essentially possessed of *atè* – this sort of transgressive desire. What Lacan is trying to imagine here – and this takes us back to the question of the philosophical death – is that this selfish obsessional character of the philosophical death could be linked perhaps to what Lacan calls the phallic function of knowledge. Death is that in relation to which one has ultimate phallic satisfaction, and so much of literature and cinema, and pornography obviously, is concerned with that phallic function of knowledge. What Lacan is interested in is that excessive dimension of *jouissance* and he calls that, with a nod towards Heidegger, *ek-sistence*, or standing out in existence. And then he makes a further remark which is very interesting – he's thinking of Kierkegaard – and he says: 'there are men who are just as good as women, namely those who get the sense that there must be *jouissance* that is beyond – those are the ones we call mystics.' Lacan is fascinated with this experience of a transgressive and excessive character of love, which exceeds knowledge, and which seems to be most powerfully articulated by female mystics. But this is something of which also men are capable – and he's thinking of Kierkegaard here.

Now, to go back to the question of love more directly: for me, the question of love is about what the poet Anne Carson has called an act of absolute spiritual daring. Carson is also fascinated with Porete; she sees her as a successor to Sappho and a precursor to someone like Simone Weil. In Carson's words, love dares the self to leave itself behind, to enter into a kind of poverty, to engage with its own annihilation. So love is an act of absolute spiritual daring that eviscerates the old self in order that something new can come into being – and this is what I think is behind this idea – to hew and hack away at oneself in order to make a space that is large enough for love to enter. What is attempted by people like Porete – and for me it is only the attempt which is interesting, not some theophanic outcome – is an act of absolute daring. Love is an act of daring where one is willing to enter into an impoverishment of the self in order to open what we might call an *immortal* dimension of subjectivity. This, for me, is a new theme and I'm not really in control of it, but it's something that interested me when I've listened to Alain Badiou over the years, where Badiou is critical of the axiom of finitude, which he thinks governs philosophy. And he talks about the possibility of eternal life, which for me makes absolutely no sense other than in this way. The only proof of immortality is an act of daring that attempts to extend beyond oneself by annihilating oneself, to project onto something that exceeds one's powers of projection. This is what I think Lacan means when he says that to love is to give what one does not have, to someone who doesn't want it. I've been thinking about the experience of love in relationship to Oscar Wilde's *De Profundis* recently and Wilde talks about love as the 'capacity to receive that over which one has no power'. So, ultimately, the problem with the philosopher is the risk of trying to reduce everything to what is in one's power, and love would be that act over which I have no power.

CC: *In your recent text,* Mystical Anarchism, *you link the model of the medieval female mystic and the heresy of the movement of the free spirit to forms of anarchism. Could you explain this relation?*

SC: For me, medieval mysticism could be linked to models of anarchism, albeit in a peculiar way – I don't deny for a second that this is weird stuff. But what Norman Cohn calls mystical anarchism, and which I try to write about, is the possibility of a sinless communion with others. Now, I have huge problems with that formulation, but I'm very intrigued by this idea that the annihilation of the self in an act of love could also be the basis for a communal experience. And in a way, both the history of heretical thought and the history of radical utopian thought have constantly gone back to this idea. Again, I have my problems with that. But to make another reference here, which I think is interesting, there's a little-known German anarchist thinker, Gustav Landauer, who is not only a huge influence on the young Benjamin, but also on Buber and Scholem and many others. And Landauer writes a text in 1901 called *Anarchic Thoughts on Anarchism*, and it's written in the context of the politics of assassination, linked to anarchism at that time. In that year, William McKinley, President of the United States, was assassinated by someone who declared himself an anarchist because he had heard a public speech of Emma Goldman; and the previous year, King Umberto I of Italy was assassinated by an alleged anarchist. And Landauer asked the question: what does anarchism have to do with politics of assassination and violence? He replies: absolutely nothing. He then develops his argument in the following way: the only violence that one should perpetrate as an anarchist is the killing of oneself. So the point, for Landauer, is not to kill others, but to kill oneself in order that a transformed relation to others becomes possible. This is what he calls, in a weird formulation, an act of inward colonization. So the basic question of anarchism here is the question of how one lives; and, moreover, how one behaves, and whether one behaves in such a way that one is willing to risk oneself in this act of love.

CC: *Two themes keep recurring: masochism and the overcoming of sin. How are these themes connected?*

SC: Let me try this. I've been trying to think about St Paul recently – because I was asked to give a talk in St Paul's Cathedral in London, on St Paul, and a number of things came up. On the one hand, Paul asks, in *Romans VII*: what is the relationship between sin and the law, and he says, 'if it had not been for the law I would not have known sin'; and he gives the example of coveting. He says that we would never have known what it is to partake in the sin of coveting if the law had not said: 'Thou shalt not covet.' So there's only sin in relation to the law and without the law sin lies dead. And this is the consequence of the fall. There was a moment prior to the fall, when we lived in paradise, when we were without sin. But as a consequence of the fall we are within the law and within sin and that is, if you like, an essentially masochistic structure. There's no way out of that loop between the law and sin.

CC: *Just to clarify, what does the law mean in this context?*

SC: The law is the commandment, what's expressed in the Old Testament. Initially, it is the prohibition not to eat the fruit of the tree of knowledge of good and evil. So, law and sin have this masochistic dialectical relationship, and for Paul that has the consequence that – he says in an amazing line – 'I do not understand my own actions.' He says, 'I don't understand the things that I want' – namely, that I want to follow the law, but, on the contrary, I continue to act out of sin. Then he says – and for me this is one of the most extraordinary phrases in Paul – 'For I do not do the good I want, but the evil that I do not want is what I do.' So the good that I want is the law, but the evil that I do is sin. So the self is stuck in this masochistic self-relation of a dialectic between law and sin. And then Paul exclaims – this would be an expression of the essentially divided nature of subjectivity – 'Wretched man that I am, who will deliver me from this body of death?' The answer to that question, of course, is Jesus Christ our Lord, namely the experience of faith. The only thing that can break the masochistic relationship of law and sin is an act of faith, and an act of faith has to be sustained by love. 'Without love I am a noisy gong or a clanging cymbal', Paul says. So faith has to be sustained by love. The act of love is an act of absolute spiritual daring and risk that opens itself to a transgressive dimension of subjectivity.

CC: *The subject of love is the divided subject?*

SC: It is the divided subject that is attempting to do something more than to dwell in division. This is complicated. There is the divided subject, who's divided between law and sin, between the legal command and the disavowal of that command. And that is the structure of the old law for Paul; and then love would be that which breaks with that dualism and risks the creation of a new subjectivity.

CC: *In Badiou, love is a condition for the event. How do you read Badiou on love?*

SC: The One becomes Two. I pledge myself in an act of love and this constitutes an event. In relationship to Paul, if faith is the moment when the subject arises from out of this fatal dialectic of law and sin, then love is what he calls the labour of the subject and the work of the subject on itself, which is what has to sustain the activity of faith. Faith on its own won't do; faith has to be underwritten by the experience of love. And love is that act of committing oneself, pledging oneself, in an act of daring, in an attempt to become something more. Is such a thing ever complete or finished? I don't think so. Love is nothing more than an activity of making a transgressive pledge, which is an openness to receive what is not in your power – I think that's the key thing. So love isn't an act of the ego – it's nothing I do – I can say that I'm in love, but the one I give up myself for, in the experience of love, is not in my control.

CC: *Can your ideas of ethics be formulated through the notion of love?*

SC: They haven't been until now, but I'm thinking about it. I've been rather silent on the question of love until the last couple of years and that's for personal reasons. The basic structure of what I'm trying to do in terms of ethics is this model of approval and demand – that's the basic conceptual structure. And I claim that every notion of morality or the good consists in a relationship to a demand, which at some level is approved. Now, the model that I propose in *Infinitely Demanding* is that the ethical subject might form itself in relation to an infinite ethical demand, which I approve – not in the sense that I approve something in a superficial way – but I make a commitment to be open to receive that demand. I'm now thinking of that as the demand that arises in the experience of faith and love, and that's something that wasn't there in *Infinitely Demanding*.

CC: *You've been speaking about the relationship between the subject and God at great length now, but you have not said much about the relationship between the subject and the other. Maybe we could move on to questions of love in relationship to another person and maybe, in addition, questions of love in relationship to our contemporary society. As you have already mentioned, we're anti-Victorians – we can speak about sex until we're blue in the face, but we can't deal with death. And what might be added to that picture is that our society is obsessed with well-being. It is obsessed with well-*

being to such extent that most practices, even sex and love, seek to improve our well-being.

SC: Yes, we live in societies where well-being has become the only legitimate end for human life. That idea of well-being is a very individualistic idea. It's not well-being linked to a collective project, as it was, for example, in communism or socialism, the building up of a New Jerusalem or something. Well-being is a personal experience of contentment; and to lead an authentic life is to achieve and cultivate well-being; and then to use certain practices as ways of achieving well-being: yoga, inner-child work, hot yoga, cold yoga, couples therapy, past-life regression and so on and so forth. I think that this is pernicious, to say the least. We're living in an age of authenticity and well-being and I want to oppose that in the most vigorous way imaginable. For me, love is an act: a trial and a struggle of which human beings are barely capable. We can dispose ourselves in such a way as to be open to the demand in relation to love but we cannot be equal to that demand. So what's at the heart of the experience of love is an experience of an infinite demand, which tears me to pieces. So the only love that is worthy of the name is a love that doesn't know itself.

CC: *But at the same time love has always had a relation to the idea of well-being, insofar as it is assumed to heal the self and make it complete.*

SC: Yes, but I completely disagree with that idea of love, that what one is looking for in love is the other half of one's being that would make one complete. This is what you find in Aristophanes' speech in the *Symposium* of Plato, where he says that we were originally beings with two faces, two arms, two legs, joined together; and we were torn apart in some sort of traumatic experience; and what we're seeking to do in love is to find that whole again. Sex is the way to rejoin with one's primal experience of the self, and I think this is ludicrous and that's one of the things that are obviously wrong with our society: the confusion of sex and love. As Socrates puts it in the *Symposium*: love is an experience of transcendence, transcendence in the sense of going beyond; love is this excessive dimension of subjectivity that is attempting to overstep itself, this *en plus* that I mentioned before, and that doesn't produce the subjective effect of well-being or the experience of an oceanic feeling, but a constant sense of failure and a painful experience of not being the equal to the demand that love makes.

My wife gave me a watch. I'm wearing it now. It's a self-winding watch, a vintage Bulova, the kind that was kept up the ass of the father of Bruce Willis's character in *Pulp Fiction* (remember that amazing scene with Christopher Walken!). Okay, I asked her to marry me in the manner of Molly Bloom's soliloquy in *Ulysses* and she gave me a watch. Engraved on the back are the words, 'Yes I said yes I will Yes'. And I have to wind this watch every day, because it constantly stops. If I don't have it on my wrist, it will stop in an hour or so. So the watch only works insofar as I vigorously shake it every day, which makes its mechanism function for another few hours. I think love is like that; love is that act of the constant shaking of oneself. So I think contentment is a selfish obsessional structure into which one slips back, and love is the countermovement to that. It's that shaking up of the subject, which forces it back into the activity of committing.

CC: *Another obvious theme in relation to love is possession: one wants to possess and one is possessed. In literature, a common picture of the lover is someone who tries to possess the beloved but ends up being possessed. Instead of overcoming an experience of jealousy, it grows stronger. I believe this is what you find in someone like Proust, where the love object, even long after her death, can provoke feelings of jealousy in the lover and a false experience of possession.*

SC: I think love is to be possessed but not to possess. One gives oneself in an act of love but one does not receive that back in equal measure; there's no guarantee. Love isn't a contract, like a marriage contract that establishes into a mutually satisfactory relationship. Love – to go back to this idea of annihilation – is the attempt to eviscerate oneself in relationship to an other who possesses you, but whom you don't possess. Or, to put it into another framework, love is an act of alienation: I alienate myself, from myself, in relationship to the alien that I love.

CC: *This idea of love as annihilation and evisceration that you describe seems somehow connected to masochism, particularly if we look at Porete and her vivid description of 'hacking and hewing away at oneself'. At the same time, the masochistic relation, at least according to Deleuze, is based on this contract, which regulates the relation between two parties; and that definition of a regulated masochism seems to have little in common with the idea that love is an act of absolute spiritual daring.*

SC: Well, I think masochism is a contract with oneself to hate oneself or to exist in this dialectic of law and sin. Love would be what attempts to break with that contract. It's not a contractual relationship between two parties; it's one party giving themselves up to something that will attempt to exceed the logic of masochism, although one slips back. I think there's an essential masochism to the structure of subjectivity and that masochism of self-satisfaction and self-loathing is what love is trying to break.

CC: *So in that sense, love is not necessarily connected to masochism?*

SC: Right.

CC: *It's a response?*

SC: Love is the attempt to break the logic of masochism that defines the subject, and to behave in a different way. That's something that has to be wound up everyday, like the watch, and it's something with no end; and it requires a constant experience of faith. That's the only sense I can make of love.

CC: *How about sex, then, as opposed to love?*

SC: There's this wonderful essay by Freud, called *The Universal Tendency Towards Debasement in the Sphere of Love,* where male sexuality is divided between sex and love in the following way: the man might love his wife but experiences impotence in his sexual relationship with her. So Freud begins this essay by saying that the most common feature he witnesses in treatment is non-organic male impotence: the man who cannot perform sexually with his wife, whom he might love, the good bourgeois wife; but with the whore or the prostitute he experiences dramatic potency, which is to say that male sexuality can achieve potency only in relation to the debased object. The woman has to be debased in order to be sexually enjoyed and that means that the debased object is no longer a person. It's an object, a thing. And I think this is the logic of pornography. Pornography is sexual gratification in relation to a debased object, and that's the problem with male sexuality. So the question is whether there could be potency of a certain sort in the experience of love. And the paradox is that the potency consists in an essential impotence; because if love is to give what one does not have, or receiving that over which one has no power, then the beloved is that which exceeds my potency, my potentiality. So there's always this delicate dialectic between potency and impotence, it seems to me. The fantasy structure of pornography with regard to male sexuality is that potency can be enjoyed in the most boring, obsessional, repetitive, masturbatory fashion, only in relation to the debased object; whether that would be the debased, sexualized woman, the child–woman, or whatever.

CC: *So male fantasy consists in sexual gratification in relation to the debased object?*

SC: I would say the illusion, rather than fantasy. And the debased object has always and everywhere to be the same and each time different. So male sexuality is essentially the Don Juan complex of enumeration. This is what you find in Don Giovanni, in the beginning of Mozart's opera, where he is enumerating his conquests in different countries, in Germany, in Italy, in Turkey and, finally, in Spain – where it's 1003. So male sexuality is reduced to a repetitive list that is always the same, and yet each time there has to be some illusion of novelty.

CC: *And what about female sexuality?*

SC: Right – about which I know nothing.

CC: *But it's clear that female sexuality holds a central and enigmatic position in philosophy or at least in psychoanalysis. Freud saying that he could never figure out what the woman wants; and Lacan famously stating that 'Woman does not exist', as well as 'There is no such thing as sexual rapport.'*

SC: There's no sexual relationship, but there's the act of love, which attempts something more, which attempts to suture that absent relationship. I'm very interested in these female mystics – I think this is another way of addressing the question – in terms of the difference between male and female mysticism. To put it in very general terms, because there are all sorts of exceptions to this, St Francis for one, we can say that the male mystic wants to experience a contemplative union with the divine – the union of the soul with the divine, usually through forms of complex linguistic operations, like negative theology – whereas female mysticism has a much more bodily relationship to the sacred. Certainly, the greatest English mystic, Julian of Norwich, experiences her visions – they are called 'shewings' – as a direct physical relationship to Christ. It's a corporeal relationship like in *The Song of Songs*: she feels the blood from Christ's wounds running down her hands, and she's experiencing some sort of sublimation of direct sexual pleasure, but it's a corporeal relation in female mysticism. Male mysticism is much more contemplative, it's much more like the idea of living divinely that one could find in *Book X* of Aristotle's *Nicomachean Ethics*, or in passages of Plato, or in Plotinus where the soul is the pearl locked within the shell of the body, and the highest bliss would be the theoretical or contemplative life, the *bios theoretikos* – which would be to live like God. I think that whole question is very differently addressed in the female mystics, and I think psychoanalysis – and I'm not an expert on psychoanalysis – has been in many ways the attempt to deal with that question, which is the question of hysteria, classically. And what the hysteric wants is love and it is that which is impossible, which makes the hysteric impossible. I'm in love with this impossibility.

Humour

CARL CEDERSTRÖM: *Humour is a recurring theme in many of your books and in 2002 you published a book dedicated exclusively to the topic of humour. Could you begin by describing how humour can be understood in relation to those other themes you've been engaged with?*

SIMON CRITCHLEY: I had this ambition at a certain point to write a book on impossible objects. These would be objects which philosophy could not exhaust, objects which refused and were refractory to philosophical categories. And the three areas I was thinking about were poetry, music and humour. You don't need a philosopher to explain music; you don't need a philosopher to explain a poem; and you don't need a philosopher to explain the nature of humour. These are practices, or activities, that seem to resist philosophical argumentation and comprehension. It was the very resistance to philosophical comprehension that first attracted me to those three areas. And I've done work on music, even made a little mid-life crisis music with my friend John Simmons, and written a little book on poetry, which we've already mentioned. But humour is maybe the theme I've gone furthest with of those three. The first thing to say is that we don't need a philosophy of humour to explain the nature of humour. And anything that a philosopher could say about humour is in a sense a priori redundant, and – again – that's what interests me. It says something about the limits of what philosophy or conceptuality can approach. Humour interests me in particular because it's a *praxis*, an actually existing social practice, it's something that we do and understand; but it's a practice which has this capacity for reflection built into it. Humour is practically enacted theory. It's an actually existing practice, that people do, which invites us to take up a theoretical view of ourselves, of others and the world. So the way I put this is that humour is a philosophical view of the world lived unphilosophically, or at least unprofessionally.

CC: *You underscore in your book that humour allows us to change the situation in which we usually find ourselves.*

SC: Yes, I think what humour does is to invert our normal understanding of things. For example, jokes tear holes in our usual views of the empirical world. When humour works, it does so by producing a disjunction between the way things are and the way they are represented by the joke. They change the situation in which we find ourselves. That could be done in a straightforward linguistic way, as when Groucho Marx says in *Duck Soup*, 'I could dance with you till the cows come home. On second thought, I'd rather dance with the cows till you come home.' There's another great Marx Brothers line, from *A Night at the Opera*, in a dialogue that goes back and forth really fast, where Chico says to Groucho: 'What'll I say?', and Groucho says, 'Tell them you're not here', and then Chico says, 'Suppose they don't believe me?', and Groucho says, 'They'll believe you when you start talking.' Or again there are examples from Beckett that I like, as in *Endgame*, when Clov asks, 'Do you believe in the life to come?' and Hamm replies, 'Mine was always that.' So humour produces this inversion; our expectations are defeated and a novel actuality is produced. As you say in your question, there's a change in the situation in which we find ourselves, and that corresponds to a very classical view of humour. You find that in Cicero, where he writes: 'The most common kind of joke is that in which we expect one thing and another is said.' And he completes the quote by saying that our 'own disappointed expectation makes us laugh'. So jokes work through a certain inversion of sense, a defeat of our expectations. Another formulation of this is from Kant, not the most humorous of philosophers, but Kant says, in the *Critique of Judgment*, that what takes place in laughter is a 'sudden evaporation of expectation into nothing'. We find this repetitive loop – usually in the form of a threefold repetition: an Englishman, an Irishman, a Scotsman, or whatever it might be – to build up expectations. So a great comic is someone who uses time in the form of repetition to tease out our expectations, and then the punch line is the evaporation of that, into nothing – and then we laugh. I think it's a powerful view, and we find an almost childlike thrill in that.

CC: *You say in your book that humour is a form of critical social anthropology. Can you explain what you mean by that?*

SC: You find some really interesting literature on humour in the area of anthropology. What you find there is the argument that jokes are rites. A rite here is understood as a symbolic act that derives its meaning from a cluster of socially legitimated symbols, like a funeral. A funeral is a rite. It involves certain things: for a funeral service, you put the body in the grave or you burn it in the crematorium – there's a priest or a pastor present, or whatever. Social life is constituted around these rites, and anthropology, when trying to read the society, reads the symbolic structure of a society, which is essentially the legibility of the rites that make up that society. Now, jokes are anti-rites that negatively show the rites that constitute a certain social system. So jokes give us an anthropologically inverted mirror image of the society that we're looking at. If we can understand how a society laughs, then, in negative relief, we can understand how society functions. So humour is a form of critical social anthropology, defamiliarizing the familiar. To understand how a society laughs is the most difficult thing to do; the most difficult thing to read about a society is its humour structure. This is why humour is so difficult to translate, and the last thing that one picks up when learning a foreign language is how jokes work; or, even more so, how to tell a joke, because you need to be inside that social structure.

CC: *I really like this example from your book that you borrow from Kundera. It's also from a funeral and it describes how a hat falls on the coffin, just as it is lowered into the grave, and at that point laughter is born. But why exactly is this funny?*

SC: Well. It's an example of how a rite becomes an anti-rite. In this way humour gives us a detailed internal anthropology of the way in which a society functions. There's something incredibly compelling about that. Joke-telling works in the following way (and this is important because it touches on Bergson's theory of laughter in his book *Laughter*): joking is a meaningful practice that the audience and the joke-teller recognize as such. So, in order for joking to work there has to be a tacit social contract, a tacit agreement about the way in which the world is organized, the way in which the world is, and it's that tacit consensus that jokes are going to play with, or fuck with. So in order for jokes to work there has to be a tacit contract, or a tacit congruence, between joke structure and social structure. There's this wonderful quotation from Bergson's *Laughter* where he says: 'To understand laughter we must put it back into its natural environment, which is society, and above all we must determine the utility of its function, which is a social one.' 'Laughter', he says, 'must answer to certain requirements of life in common; it must have a social signification.' This goes back to the idea that what's going on in jokes, laughter and humour requires an understanding of *sensus communis*, common sense; or, better translated, sociability. Humour requires sociability. The basic claim I'm making is that, on the one hand, humour requires this tacit social agreement, this basic sociability, this *sensus communis*; and the way in which great humour works is by producing a dissensus within the common. It produces something which pushes against our basic mode of sociability: something shocking, even offensive. That's why offensive humour is so important, because it reveals the nature of the mores and symbolic structures that constitute our social life.

CC: *And reactionary humour would be the opposite?*

SC: Reactionary humour is incredibly interesting, for all the wrong reasons. Most humour is reactionary to start with. Most humour isn't very good. A distinction you have to make – and which I'm happy to make – is the distinction between good and bad humour. You can't just have a phenomenological description of humour; you also need to have a normative claim driving that description. My very simple normative claim is that good humour is laughing at yourself and bad humour is laughing at others. Reactionary humour in that sense would be bad humour, which consists in laughing at others, and the way in which that works most obviously is in ethnic humour. I could say a word about that.

CC: *Please do.*

SC: Much humour simply seeks to confirm the status quo, either by denigrating a certain sector of society, like sexist jokes about women, or by laughing at the alleged stupidity of a social outsider, such as jokes about foreigners. So reactionary humour, in the form of ethnic humour, takes the form of the identification of an outsider who is scapegoated. The scapegoated outsider takes on two forms: either the stupid outsider or the clever outsider. It's usually the stupid out-sider. So if we think about ethnic jokes – the British laugh at the Irish, the Canadians laugh at the Newfoundlanders, the Americans laugh at the Poles (or they used to). There's that awful old American joke: 'How can you tell who's the wife at a Polish wedding? She's the one wearing the clean bowling shirt.' The Swedes laugh at the Norwegians, the Finns laugh at the Swedes. The Greeks laugh at the Pontians, the Czechs laugh at the Slovaks, the Russians laugh at the Ukrainians, the French laugh at the Belgians, the Dutch also laugh at the Belgians – and everybody laughs, rather nervously, at the Germans. The Germans are a special case, which is captured in the idea of the humourless German. There's a great joke about German food: 'The food is great, but an hour later you're hungry for power.' This is a brilliant joke; it's actu-ally a meta-joke because the joke is the joke about Chinese food – 'You like Chinese food, but an hour later you're hungry again' – that becomes the basis for the meta-joke about German food. Now, in the German context we can go back 200 years to figures like the German Romantic writer Jean Paul, writing in the early nineteenth century, and he says that the Germans have a problem with humour. The exem-plary case of the Germans is one where they see themselves as having a problem with humour, and obviously, since the Second World War, that has become an even more egregious problem. Most cultures think of themselves as funny, and the way in which their humour works is by laughing at others. The Germans have the unique virtue of often not finding themselves funny and finding humour a problem, which of course makes them even funnier.

CC: *Another aspect of humour – which I think is closely connected to ethnic humour – is that it becomes a social structure through which a group can organize its enjoyment. And this is often connected to the figure of the other, or the obscene other that somehow repulses us.*

SC: Yes, you enjoy the suffering of the other by marking them as stupid outsiders. Obviously, if we think about basic racist humour, it's usually the stupid foreigner or the stupid black guy. That's one side, and that's a way of organizing enjoyment, absolutely. The first theory of humour – and there are mainly three major theories of humour, and we can come back to that in a moment – is what John Morreall calls the superiority theory. The superiority theory of humour is very simple: we laugh out of the feeling of superiority over others. And this theory you can find in Plato, Aristotle, Quintilian and, at the dawn of the modern era, Hobbes. Hobbes has a fascinating remark on laughter in *Leviathan* where he says that laughter is 'sudden glory arising from a sudden conception of some eminency in our selves by comparison with the infirmities of others or with our own formerly'. 'Laughter', Hobbes says, 'is that passion which has no name', a nameless passion which arises from the experience of superiority over others. Hobbes thought that humour was extremely dangerous and had to be managed, had to be organized. You can take that back to Plato. Plato similarly thought that the core of laughter consisted in feelings of superiority over others. Therefore, when he was imagining the guardians of the philosophical city in the *Republic*, he said that they shouldn't be allowed to laugh. And you find that in different ways in the Christian tradition. In early Christianity, when the monastic tradition begins, monks were not allowed to laugh, and then a few centuries later they were allowed to smile in certain ways; but laughter had to be restrained – it was seen as evil.

Now, to come back to reactionary humour, or rather ethnic humour, I would say that ethnic humour is a powerful confirmation of the superiority theory of humour. The other way in which ethnic humour works is by identifying not just the stupid outsider, but the clever outsider. For example, anti-Scottish jokes are usually about the Scot being excessively canny or clever, and that is usually linked to them being mean with money. Or indeed anti-Semitic humour has the same structure, with jokes about Jews being too clever or being excessively mean with money. So the identification of an other that you can laugh at – both in the form of the excessively stupid other, and the excessively clever other – is a way of marking the boundary of a society.

CC: *That's one aspect of it, certainly. However, I guess there's also much to be learnt from the way in which we use the other in order to escape our own shortcomings. Surely, the other is the perfect alibi for covering over these shortcomings. But in that way, we might also read ethnic humour symptomatically insofar as it reveals our inability to be what we want to be.*

SC: Yes, and in a perverse way I want to defend ethnic humour. It gives the lie to the idea that we live in some global liberal cosmopolitan order where we all get along. Actually, what we laugh at has a strangely regressive structure. Our patterns of humour correspond to forms of national identity: in the case of Europe, which I know best, they are rather antique to say the least; they go back to stereotypes which people no longer really believe in, but they live on in humour. So humour, in this sense, has this sort of delayed effect, an essential anachronism. I think that ethnic humour is hugely important because it allows us to reflect on the anxious nature of our thrownness in the world. We're thrown into the world, in the Heideggerian sense, with a set of prejudices that make up the social system of which we're a part, and ethnic humour lets us see our captivity within those structures. So, if you like, to put it in a more philosophical form: in its untruth, reactionary humour tells us important truths about who we are. So jokes – ethnic jokes, racist jokes – can therefore be read as symptoms of societal repression and the eruption of those jokes can be seen as a return of the repressed. To that extent, ethnic humour reveals to us that we're persons that we'd rather not be, and this corresponds roughly to the argument of Freud's book on *Witz, Jokes and their Relation to the Unconscious*, from 1905. For Freud, what's going on in jokes is the articulation of repressed unconscious content. So what you can read in the joke is what is being repressed by that society. This obviously works in relation to ethnic and racist humour, but also sexist humour. An example would be: you're in a bar and someone is telling a series of relatively unfunny homophobic jokes. If you were Freud you'd say: 'Aha, these jokes are symptoms of the man's repression of latent homosexuality.' You read the joke as a symptom of repression, and there's a lot to that. So ethnic humour, if you like, negatively reveals the repressed content of a certain society. It reveals that we're people that we'd rather not be. We might like to think of ourselves as these cosmopolitan liberals, but actually we're those dreadful racist, sexist creatures, whose economy of enjoyment, as you say, is bound up with laughing at others.

CC: *You describe humour as embedded in social structures, and I agree with that. But I think we could also see an invasion of what might be called a global humour. What I have in mind are all these sit-coms, like* Friends, *which try to reach as large an audience as possible.*

SC: I don't know if there's a globalization of humour. You can say there's the *imperialism* of American, popular culture which functions through the transmission of certain shows, like *Friends*, which I think is deeply, deeply, unfunny (I've watched it a lot with my son). The first thing to point out is that there's very little of what I call true humour – and I'll come back to what that means later on – in shows like *Friends*. Such shows simply serve to buttress the social mores and conventions of existing society. It's not humour.

CC: *Humour for passive nihilists?*

SC: The passive nihilist finds everything funny; it's a form of complete self-protection. You see this on American late night television. For me it's completely uninteresting other than reading it diagnostically.

CC: *Let's move away from this subject and back to humour. You began describing three forms of humour.*

SC: Yes. First there's the superiority theory: that one laughs at a feeling of superiority over others. Someone walks in the room, they trip up and fall over, and you laugh at them. The second theory is the relief theory, which claims that what's going on in humour is the release of pent-up nervous energy. This theory goes back to Herbert Spencer in the mid nineteenth century, and it's that theory that Freud is propagating in *Jokes and Their Relation to the Unconscious*. Freud's argument in that book is that the energy that is relieved and discharged in laughter produces pleasure because it allegedly economizes on the energy that would ordinarily be used to contain or repress psychic activity. Humour in that sense is comic relief. It's like masturbation, but slightly more acceptable to perform in public; it's a form of discharge of energy. For me, the most interesting theory of humour, and the one that I want to defend in a modified form, is the incongruity theory. This theory can be traced back to Francis Hutcheson, the great Irish-Scottish philosopher from the early eighteenth century, and it's elaborated in people like Kant, Schopenhauer and Kierkegaard. The way in which the incongruity theory works is that humour is produced through a felt incongruity between what we know or expect to be the case, and what takes place in the joke. That is, the joke works through the production of incongruity between expectation and actuality. So a great comic is able to use that incongruity to shake up the way we see things.

CC: *So this is what you find in true humour?*

SC: Yes, but I would say that 99 per cent of humour is the comedy of recognition; it simply buttresses existing prejudices and makes us feel better about ourselves. Or it's comic relief, a transient corporeal affect. What the incongruity theory allows us to see is something more going on in humour. There's a quotation that I really like. It's from Trevor Griffiths, from his wonderful 1975 play *Comedians*, which is about a comedian called Eddie Waters who's running a comedy class in Manchester, and he's trying to teach people to be funny – a hard thing to do. He says, and this is the quote:

> A real comedian – that's a daring man. He *dares* to see what his listeners shy away from, fear to express. And what he sees is a sort of truth, about people, about their situation, about what hurts or terrifies them, about what's hard, above all about what they *want*. A joke releases the tension, says the unsayable, any joke pretty well. But a true joke, a comedian's joke, has to do more than release tension, it has to *liberate* the will and the desire, it has to *change the situation*.

So any joke can release tension. But a comedian's joke, a true joke, has to do more than that: it has to change the situation in which we find ourselves. So, a great joke lets us see the familiar defamilarized, lets us see the ordinary rendered extraordinary, and we laugh with a sort of squeal of delight. This is why the surrealists were so interested in humour. André Breton put together his anthology on black humour, *L'Humour noir*, in 1940. And he was thinking specifically about Jonathan Swift's wonderful 'Modest Proposal', from the 1720s, where Swift proposes that the way in which we're going to solve the problem of poverty in Ireland is by killing Irish children and feeding them to the English and then goes through various recipes that could be used for cooking young Irish children and enjoying a delicious meal. What Swift is engaged in there is a lacerating critique of the inhuman way in which the English were treating the Irish at that point in history. Kafka would be another wonderful example of black humour: you wake one morning to find that you've suddenly been turned into a huge beetle. This would be the idea of humour as a 'surrealization' of the real. And for me that's the important aspect of humour.

CC: *When you go into the subject of black humour in your book, you do so in relationship to Freud. You claim that true humour allows us to laugh at ourselves even in the most morbid and hopeless situations. Could you explain this connection between black humour and laughing at oneself?*

SC: As I said before, Freud wrote the book on *Witz* in 1905 and he didn't go back to the topic until 1927 when he writes a very brief essay, it's just a few pages, called '*Der Humor*'. For me, this is an absolutely fascinating paper. Freud begins with an empirical example, as he often does, and he lets the empirical example have its effect. People always get Freud wrong. Freud is not some clumsy, dogmatic theorist; he's constantly changing his theoretical views based on the different empirical data that he's presented with. The empirical datum in this essay is a joke, and Freud collected jokes for his whole life. It is about a condemned man who, on the morning of his execution, leaves his cell, walks out into the courtyard, sees the gallows ahead of him, sees his fate, looks up at the sky and says: 'Well, the week's beginning nicely.' And Freud says that what's going on in this joke is that the condemned man, who's going to die, looks at himself from outside of himself and finds himself ridiculous – that's the essential insight. So humour consists in looking at oneself from outside oneself and finding oneself ridiculous. And the effect of finding oneself ridiculous in that manner, Freud says, is *befreiend* and *erhebend* (liberating and elevating).

This is complicated because there's no suggestion that the man is going to be liberated or freed; no, he's going to be hanged by his neck, until he expires. But the effect of this humour is to liberate and elevate his situation by looking at himself from outside of himself and finding himself ridiculous. Then Freud derives his theoretical consequence from this example. He backs up and says the superego, or the 'Over-I' – *das Über-Ich* in German – is a very peculiar thing. In the analytic situation we're presented with the omnipresence of that superego. It's the superego, or what he calls in his 1914 essay *On Narcissism*, conscience. It's conscience that lacerates us and makes us prisoners to ourselves and makes us suffer from our symptoms. And that superego is that place where our mother, our father, our authority figures, our hated figures – they all gather and group in there and they make you feel like a worthless piece of shit that does not deserve to live. The superego is what the analyst has to replace in order for psychoanalysis to take place. The place of the superego has to be given over to the analyst in order for analytic work to be done on the symptoms. Psychoanalysis knows that the superego is a dangerous animal, especially when caged. What's revealed in humour is another form of superego, a superego that doesn't just lacerate and condemn, but a superego that looks at us from outside of ourselves, and gives us the occasion for humour – for mirth of some kind. This, he says, reveals a more benign function for the superego. I take that line of argument in Freud and then make a distinction between two forms of superego, what I call, with devastating neologistic deftness, Superego I and Superego II. Superego I is the lacerating superego that tells you you're a worthless piece of shit. Superego II is this more benign superego. And you can say that these two versions of the superego correspond to its infantile and mature forms. That lacerating superego is the superego of the child being told not to touch itself when it goes to bed at night, or whatever. Superego II on the other hand is a mature superego that is capable of looking at itself from outside of itself and finding itself ridiculous. And that superego is your amigo – that's my claim. What that reveals is something really interesting: conscience, which makes cowards of us all, is not just a negative thing. Conscience can be something else.

CC: *In* Infinitely Demanding *you raise the claim that conscience and humour – mediated through the Superego II – can be seen as a novel model for ethical subjectivity. Could you develop this argument?*

SC: The argument in *Infinitely Demanding* is that the source of ethical motivation in the subject is an infinite ethical demand, which produces a splitting, a division, within the subject and the objection that can be raised against that is the following: what prevents that form of infinite ethical demand from simply being bad conscience in the way that Nietzsche talks about it in the *Genealogy of Morals*, as the vivisection of the self. And my response is to try and give a whole theory of sublimation, which I don't need to go into now. But for me, humour gives us a powerful discourse of sublimation that allows us both to maintain the infinite ethical demand and to moderate and assuage that demand. And if there's a complaint I have about the reception of *Infinitely Demanding* then it is that no one really picked up on these arguments and we ended up with fairly stupid objections to my understanding of politics and resistance. For me this is a key insight: that the infinite ethical demand is something which needs to be sublimated through an experience of humour – this ability to look at oneself from outside of oneself. Now, to go back more directly to the question of humour, there's an old German expression that I know from the work of Helmuth Plessner, a philosophical anthropologist – really interesting. He wrote a book called *Laughing and Crying* and then another wonderful essay called 'Das Lächeln' ('The Smile'). The German expression is *Ich bin, aber ich habe mich nicht* ('I am, but I do not have myself'). And his claim – and I think he's right – is that the human is essentially *eccentric*. He says that the animal is what it is: a cat is a cat, a goldfish is a goldfish. But a human being is *not* what it is. A human being *is* something, sure, but then it has a relationship of having to itself that produces a disjunction at its heart. We can call that the experience of self-consciousness, the experience of a division between the soul and the body, or however you want to play that out. But there is an essential division at the heart of the human being. The human being is eccentric with regard to itself. It's eccentric with regard to its material nature. And this can be confirmed by looking at two areas of humour: the relationship between humans and animals in jokes, and the relationship to the body.

Let me explain what I mean here. There are an awful lot of jokes about animals, but I would argue that they take two main forms. There are jokes when the animal becomes human and there are jokes when human becomes animal. When the animal becomes human, the effect is surprising, pleasing, diverting – my favourite joke in this regard is this bear joke (I love bear jokes – I loved Herzog's *Grizzly Man*) that I recount in the book on humour, where the hunter goes into the woods to hunt a bear. He's waiting by the side of the clearing; the bear appears, runs towards him, screaming – or whatever noise bears make – the hunter shoots his rifle, it jams, and the bear viciously sodomizes him, leaves him on the ground and disappears back into the woods; and the man is really angry. Next day, the hunter goes back with a new rifle, same situation arises: the bear comes out of the wood – it's three o'clock in the afternoon – the hunter takes his rifle, shoots, the rifle jams again, the bear flips him over, sodomizes him, leaves him on the ground. And by this time the man is absolutely furious. He drives back into the city, buys an AK-47 assault rifle, goes back the next day, same spot, three o'clock in the afternoon, the bear comes out of the woods; the man takes his AK-47 assault rifle, aims at the bear, and unbelievably the thing jams again. And the bear turns to the man, puts his hands on the shoulders and says: 'Look, this isn't really about hunting, is it?' What happens there is that the animal becomes human and the effect is pleasing, diverting, surprising.

CC: *And when the human becomes animal?*

SC: When the human becomes animal, the effect is disgusting. A great example of this would be, once again, from one of my heroes, Jonathan Swift, from *Gulliver's Travels* Book IV, *Voyage to the Land of the Houyhnhnms*. The Houyhnhnms are rational animals. They are horses, who discourse with themselves and have elegant conversations, while living in a tolerant and well-organized society (it's a little like Sweden). Swift's point is that if the human being is understood to be a rational animal, then why not a talking horse? By contrast there are these creatures in trees, called 'Yahoos', and the Yahoos are degraded human beings. They have become bestial: they sit in trees, they shit on the ground, they shit on the horses and randomly fuck each other, eating raw food or whatever. The effect of the human becoming animal is disgusting. And that corresponds to two genres of satire: Horatian satire, which plays with the foibles of everyday life. A good example here would be Alexander Pope's *The Rape of the Lock*, where he constructs what was called in the eighteenth century mock-heroic verse, whereby the techniques of Homeric and Virgilian epic are used to describe the loss of a piece of hair by an aristocratic lady. That's mock-heroic, light, Horatian satire. The other tradition is Juvenalian satire, which is about travesty. It's about the human being, being degraded, and the effect is sort of disgusting. But for me, what those two forms of satire reveal is not that the human being cannot be an animal, or that an animal cannot be human. Rather, it reveals that the human cannot be human. And that is also what is really funny, when a human being tries too hard to be human. There are various forms of humour that depict that very well. And this goes back to another remark of Bergson's. He says that what's funny is when the organic becomes mechanical; when a human being begins to resemble a machine, that's funny. We can think of that in relationship to silent movies, where human beings take on a machine-like, repetitive aspect. In its most extreme form, we find this in Chaplin's *Modern Times* where the tramp character becomes part of the industrial mechanized process, becomes a machine – we find that funny. This idea that there's an essential eccentricity at the heart of the human being's relation to itself.

CC: *Laughter and humour also bear a close relation to the body. You point out that it is a bodily phenomenon but that it cannot be reduced to a bodily phenomenon. Could you elaborate on these thoughts?*

SC: Laughter is one of the three activities that can be described as explosions expressed with the body, where the body seems to override the mind or consciousness. The other two would be excessive crying – weeping or sobbing – and orgasm, obviously. Laughter is a muscular phenomenon consisting of the spasmodic contraction and relaxation of the facial muscles with corresponding movements of the diaphragm – that's what laughter is: it's a physical eruption. For me, what's essential is the division between that material aspect of laughter and its social meaning. For example, if laughter consists in an explosion expressed with the body and the bearing of teeth, that might have the social meaning of laughter for us; in another context that might have the meaning of aggression or sexual threat. If a dog or a monkey bears its teeth, then it's either going to try to bite you or fuck you – or maybe both. Laughter is a bodily phenomenon, but it cannot be reduced to the body. There is an opinion out there, usually associated with Bakhtin's *Rabelais and His World*, which is a fantastic book, that laughter is an eruption of what Bakhtin calls 'the lower-bodily-material stratum'. The truth of laughter is the expressiveness of the body. You also get this idea in Bataille and elsewhere. I think this is just wrong. I mean, what laughter reveals is the disjunction between mind and body, or the disjunction between consciousness and materiality – which goes back to this idea that 'I am but I do not have myself'. What goes on in laughter is not the identification of myself with my body, but the experience of a division between myself and my body. That I cannot be my body and that my body cannot be me. Humour is a weird confirmation of mind–body dualism.

CC: *So true humour not only changes the situation; it also underscores human beings' inescapable self-division.*

SC: Yes. For me the essential take-away message from my view of humour is that, at its best, as in, say, the Marx Brothers, humour is a series of verbal inversions and distortions that can bring about a change in the situation in which we find ourselves; and which gives us a way of looking at ourselves from outside ourselves and finding ourselves ridiculous; and which allow us to bear the weight of the ethical demand and at the same point to wear it with a sort of lightness. There's a great joke, another Groucho Marx joke, which I think reveals the situation of humour perfectly. It's a Grock joke, about the man who has lost his will to live, and goes to see a psychoanalyst. The analyst has a few sessions with him, but he's making no progress; in fact he's getting worse. One day the analyst says to him at the end of the session, 'Look, tonight, for the first time in an awful long time, the greatest comedian in the world, Grock, is in town, he's performing tonight. I would suggest you go along and see him; it might make you feel better.' The patient says nothing. It's the end of the session. He gets up, walks towards the door and the analyst says, 'By the way, what's your name again?'. And the patient says, 'I am Grock.' What that reveals is that, yes, one has lost the will to live; yes, one is suffering, but the joke gives you an ability to sublimate that, to bear it, to acknowledge it. This goes back to questions of tragedy, comedy and humour.

CC: *That's something I would like to speak more about; the relationship between what you call in* Infinitely Demanding *tragic affirmation and comic acknowledgement.*

SC: This began in the late 1990s, when I discovered the Freud essay on humour, when I was living in Germany. It was a revelation. At the same time I was getting very interested in the relationship between ethics and sublimation, and reading Lacan's *Ethics of Psychoanalysis* and trying to make links between that and the work of Levinas. Those essays came out in *Ethics – Politics – Subjectivity* in 1999. There's an essay in that book where I try and develop two paradigms for thinking about sublimation. If sublimation in Freudian terms is the transformation of the object at which the drive aims, then to link that to a Lacanian formula, it is the 'elevation of the object to the dignity of the Thing'. The model of sublimation for Lacan is tragedy, not just tragedy – Lacan is very funny. There's much to be said about Lacan's relation to humour, because it's profound. But in the *Ethics of Psychoanalysis*, the heroine of psychoanalysis is Antigone, and Antigone is the tragic heroine who does not give way on her desire. She takes that desire all the way to death. What you have in Lacan is a model of tragic sublimation and I try to develop a history of the privileging of the tragic in post-Kantian philosophy. This really begins in Schelling, in his *Letters on Dogmatism and Criticism*, from 1796, and is then developed later on in his *Philosophy of Art*. Schelling's idea is that what is sublime in tragedy is the possibility of a reconciliation between the orders of freedom and necessity: freedom in the subject, and necessity in the object. And tragedy – and he's thinking in particular of the tragedy of Sophocles: *Oedipus the King* or *Oedipus Rex* – allows us to imagine a momentary harmonization of those orders. So Oedipus is free; he believes himself free at the beginning of the tragedy. The process of the tragedy is the unfolding of the captivity of Oedipus by necessity. It was ordained by fate that he should murder his father and marry his mother. The unravelling of the play is the unravelling of the illusion of freedom and the captivity of Oedipus by necessity. So in what does the sublimity of tragedy consist? Schelling says that what's sublime here is Oedipus' free recognition of the determination of his being by necessity – he accepts that. Now, if we fast-forward 130 years to Heidegger, we find a very similar claim being made in *Being and Time* in 1927, and then later on in *The Introduction to Metaphysics* in 1935. In *Being and Time*, being-towards-death is my free responsibility towards my fate: death is death, it is necessary, it's my fate; what's sublime in human existence is the ability to affirm that being-towards-death, and to make being-towards-death the condition of possibility for authenticity. It's that model that finds its way into Lacan's *Ethics of Psychoanalysis*. So I call this the tragic-heroic paradigm. I then began to ponder whether there could be another way of looking at this, and try to develop a comic anti-heroic paradigm, using figures like Jonathan Swift and Laurence Sterne, and moving forward eventually to figures like Beckett. What goes on in the comic situation is the inability to achieve any affirmation or momentary union between freedom and necessity; what comedy is about is the acknowledgement of the separation between freedom and necessity. Freedom simply consists in the acknowledgement of my determination by fate in a way that I cannot internalize, that I cannot make my own. Therefore, authenticity as a project is unattainable and should be given up.

CC: *To go back a little, and to ask a more elementary question about conceptuality: you write about humour and not comedy; and while I understand that it could be difficult theoretically to separate them from one another, I wonder how you deal with these two concepts and why you chose to write a book on humour instead of on comedy.*

SC: Classically, there are three aesthetic genres: the epic, the lyric and the dramatic. These three can be defined more or less well. You can define the epic in relationship to Homer, Virgil, Milton; the dramatic in relationship to Aeschylus, Sophocles, Shakespeare and all the rest. In Hegel's *Aesthetics* we have the most compelling taxonomy of those genres. The serious aesthetic genres are relatively stable. But the non-serious genres – irony, wit, humour, comedy – are incredibly difficult to define. Wherever you look, you find different definitions. Originally, the book on humour began as a book on comedy. But I realized I just couldn't fix the object: comedy was just too elusive and too big a topic to get a grip on. Humour is a little bit different. It originally refers to the doctrine of the four humours that constitute the human organism according to classical Hellenistic medicine.

In the English language, the first use of the term humour, as referring to something jocular or funny, occurs at the end of the seventeenth century, in 1682 according to the *Oxford English Dictionary*. This is why, in the eighteenth century, the French and the Germans identified humour with the English, as a form of activity that is particular to *l'esprit anglais*, as Diderot says. Humour is a relatively stable object. You can date it historically and conceptually.

CC: *A couple of years before the publication of* On Humour*, you wrote about humour, wit and irony in* Very Little . . . Almost Nothing*, in relationship to Jena Romanticism and the fragment. Could you explain the difference between these concepts?*

SC: Wit (or *Witz*) is linked to knowledge (*Wissen*), insofar as knowledge, in the Kantian formulation, means the ability to synthesize, to put together, to place an intuition under a concept. So, wit is a chemical capacity. Irony, on the other hand, means division. Irony for the early German Romantics is the expression of the separation between the self and the absolute. What's going on in the German Romantics is a theory of irony and a theory of wit. This finds expression in the genre of the fragment, cultivated with formidable power by Friedrich Schlegel and Novalis. The fragment is that form which is like a perfect mini-system. Schlegel refers to the fragment as a hedgehog – perfectly round and complete in itself. That would be the witty fragment. But within that fragment there is something that cannot be retained, an ironic moment that cannot be totalized. The fragment is both this mini-system that expresses absolute knowledge as absolute wit, and it is also the expression of the impossibility of absolute knowledge at the same time. So fragments are these simultaneously closed and open structures. Again, and back to humour, I think this is what great jokes do. Great jokes are, as it were, both perfectly closed systems and open at the same time. In that Grock joke, we know that something is going to happen – it's a form of knowledge as wit – and at the same time the punch line of the joke opens an ironic sort of dehiscence, or division, that invites us to reflect and maybe even smile.

CC: *To summarize some of your arguments, it seems as if humour emerges from an acknowledgment of sin, or the sin of the world. At the same time, the notion of sin is something you find in the texts of Carl Schmitt, and the medieval mystics – which you spoke about in the previous chapter – and these are people who are not particularly humorous. So I wondered if you could say some last words about the relationship between original sin and humour, especially how one might establish a so-called sinless communion based on a notion of comedy.*

SC: Right. There was no humour in paradise. They were probably smiling a lot, and they were conscious – but whether they were self-conscious we don't know. But it's doubtful whether the Grock joke would have got much of a laugh in the Garden of Eden. In a sinless condition, humour is absent. The conclusion is that humour is a consequence of original sin. Everything I've been saying so far about the human being – that the human being is an eccentric being, that the human being is divided from itself – means that we are ontologically defective. There's just something fucked up about being human. Sin is a name for that ontological defectiveness or fallenness or facticity, or whatever we call it. Humour arises in that situation where the human being is defined by whatever we call sin. And it gives us an ability both to understand our defectiveness and alleviate it. My interest in what I call mystical anarchism is complicated. I'm hugely attracted to those political theories, or theories of the political, that would be based on some conception of original sin – Carl Schmitt, Joseph de Maistre and then a more recent version of that would be someone like John Gray, author of *Straw Dogs* and *Black Mass*. John Gray's argument is that human beings are rapacious animals, who are driven by a lust for violence and cruelty. And the reason for that is Darwinian; the evolutionary fact about human beings is that we are rapacious animals and that's the way we have evolved and that's the way we have adapted to the environment. This is a Darwinian naturalization of original sin.

I'm very attracted to that, but suspicious and critical of its political consequences, which seem to be, in Schmitt, an argument for authoritarianism – ultimately dictatorship – and in Gray an argument for what he calls political realism. By this he means something like Edmund Burke's classical Toryism, based on the idea that the social and political order we have is not perfect, but it's the best that we're capable of, and the last thing we should do is to throw that away; therefore, revolution is a mistake, because when you have a revolution you destroy the existing traditions that underwrite liberty and you'll end up with a power vacuum into which a dictator will appear. This is the Burkean reading of the French Revolution, which, of course, was right as Hegel showed in the *Phenomenology of Spirit*. So, on the one hand, I'm attracted by those theories, but worried by their political consequences. On the other hand, I'm intrigued by this tradition of mystical anarchism, which for me is the name for a utopian, communist habit of thought that arises in these medieval heresies like the movement of the free spirit and which I think you can trace all the way through to forms of nineteenth-century utopian socialism and communism; but also to certain theories of anarchism, and groups like the situationists in the 1960s (see Raoul Vaneigem's *The Movement of the Free Spirit*), and contemporary movements like the Invisible Committee in *The Coming Insurrection* and the numerous activist and student groups that the latter have inspired. What is being offered there, as a possibility, is a form of community that would be based on a sinless union with others – a form of communism, where we are willing to throw off our defectiveness and to become perfect. This is great, but it's not funny.

Authenticity

with Tom McCarthy

CARL CEDERSTRÖM: *Two recurring themes in your work – and particularly the work that you have done in the name of the International Necronautical Society (INS) – are the themes of death and authenticity. But you seem to take up a critical attitude towards these issues, arguing against the possibility of authenticity and against the possibility of an authentic death.*

TOM MCCARTHY: Well, I think the real question, for us, is the question of the subject: the question of the self. So, for example, in the heroic tradition in literature, which pits the self against death in a way that produces authenticity, you find a hero that runs into death like a fly slamming into an electric field, and which goes out in a tremendous spark of authentic apotheosis. There's a lot about that, aesthetically, which is very seductive. However, we at the INS strongly reject that. Instead, we feel more seduced by the comic tradition in which the fly can't even reach the electric field. It keeps tripping over its legs, or becomes distracted by something – dog shit, for example. So death in the comic tradition is not that of authentic self-mastery, but rather of a slippage; it's about the inability to be oneself, and to become what one wants to be. And we think that that kind of tradition or logic is much more rich and fruitful.

SIMON CRITCHLEY: Woody Allen defines comedy as tragedy plus time, which would mean that the tragic death is the death at the right time. In comedy you don't die, and that's what's funny and even more tragic. You find this in Beckett, where the character is dying, but can't die. We're exploring the opposite to the heroic idea of death that you find in the futurists, Ernst Jünger or Heidegger, where death is an act of virile self-assertion, of shattering oneself against death, which then becomes the possibility for authenticity. What death reveals is the radical inauthenticity that's constitutive of the self. So in the comic tradition it's impossible to die authentically.

TMcC: The default mode is to be tragic, that's the thing to be. But what you get in Faulkner or Conrad – and in Beckett of course – is this failure to be tragic. In *Nostromo*, Conrad's epic, the tragic hero with the same name is meant to die, and everyone thinks he's dead. But then it turns out that there was a mix-up, and that Nostromo didn't 'get dead'. Instead, he's just wandering around town, looking different, while everyone is praising him. And meanwhile you've got the character Martin Decoud, the great European intellectual, who wants to possess the moment of his death. He shoots himself in the heart – like Conrad did – and even though he does die, he doesn't die properly, which means that not even a medical death is enough.

CC: *Another example is from a stand-up routine by Woody Allen – and it was you, Simon, who first brought my attention to this – where a man is about to drown and, just as he's expecting to see this panoramic vision summing up his entire life, he realizes that the tapes got mixed up and there's someone else's life being played out. What about this desire to witness one's own death?*

SC: There's certainly a fantasy about coinciding with oneself at the moment of one's death. You find this in Blanchot's *L'Instant de ma mort* (*The Instant of My Death*), where he talks about the time when he was nearly executed by German soldiers – actually, it might be Russian soldiers – it's all very confusing in the narrative. At the moment when the gun is being pointed at him and he's going to die he feels lightness and exhilaration. And then for some reason – it's not clear – he's not killed. The fantasy is that of coinciding with myself at the point of my death. It's the fantasy of being there, at the moment of my death, as I go out in a blaze of light. But what defines the subject for us in the INS is the absence of that self-coincidence, which is another way of thinking about inauthenticity or what we call dividualism.

TMcC: It's like Conrad, in *Nostromo*, again, he almost coincides with *the* moment. Blanchot says that the instant of my death is from now on deferred. Brilliant passage. I re-enacted it, I plagiarized it in our 'Declaration on Inauthenticity'.

SC: Another, sort of inverted version, of that fantasy would be the fantasy that you find at the end of Flaubert's *The Temptation of St Anthony* where the last temptation that appears to Flaubert is the temptation of Spinoza's God – or the devil, in the guise of Spinoza's God – that tempts Anthony with the thought that the universe is simply the infinite extension of matter. And then Anthony says at a certain point, 'Do you mean that extension could be part of God and God could be part of extension, in the infinity of matter?' and the devil says 'yes' and at the end of the novel Anthony's final fantasy is the fantasy of being matter, of unifying with matter. But we can't even do that. That coincidence is also not possible. The fantasy of becoming matter is also a theological fantasy, which brings us back to the question of the comic. Whatever we are, we are these dividuals who lack this ability to coincide with ourselves and for whom there will always be a remainder, a piece of debris.

CC: *Another image I'm thinking of here is from your book, Tom,* Men in Space, *where a cosmonaut is sent up in space just before the collapse of the Soviet Union. And after it has collapsed no one wants to be associated with him. The Russians say he belongs to Ukraine, because it was the place from which he was launched; the Ukrainians say it's a question for Estonia, because that's where he was born.*

TMcC: That's actually a real story.

SC: Could I talk about that? *Men in Space* is about – well – men in space. It's about men drifting through space with all markers of certainty having disappeared. You've got the figure of the cosmonaut adrift, without even the Soviet Union to return to; the country that he left has disappeared in the meantime. There's a sense in which people drift through the debris of an inauthentic world, a world that has obviously fallen apart, is still falling apart, leading inauthentic lives, where death is something that comes to you like feeling a twig brush against your back.

TMcC: Yes. When Anton Markov, one of the book's characters, is being shot he thinks it's a twig; he doesn't even know he's dying.

SC: The way I see it, there's something sort of flat, unreal and dematerialized about the universe in *Men in Space*. The key figure for this inauthentic world is the ellipsis, rather than the perfect circle, and we talked about that in relation to failed transcendence in our Declaration.

CC: *What about the ellipsis?*

TMcC: That came straight from Derrida: The ellipsis instead of the plenitude and perfection. The ellipsis is this mark of a lack, of disappearance, or of aporia.

SC: God isn't represented by a circle, which would denote transcendence and plenitude, but by an ellipsis, an absence, denoting failed transcendence.

TMcC: Yes. God would be like a rocket sent up, hopefully to go into orbit, to transcend the world. But it's when that rocket blows up, like the Challenger, and debris came scattering down everywhere, that it gets interesting. That's what we'd like to see. The philosophical tradition that I find inspiration from – and I'm not a proper philosopher, as Simon is: I read philosophy from the viewpoint of a novelist – is this anti-Hegelian tradition. Hegel's notion of *Aufhebung* would be like that rocket lifting everything up, sublimating it. It's about God: pure thought, pure concept. And against that you get someone like Bataille, who kind of plays the film backwards, and instead of matter going up and dematerializing, you get the exact opposite. You find this in Nietzsche as well: God's bleeding, God's smelling, God's decomposing. And the landscape that we as artists or thinkers or whatever have to deal with becomes the landscape of excrement.

CC: *This anti-Hegelian tradition seems to be of central importance to your work.*

SC: Yes. The first time I responded to Tom was in 2002, in a text called *Navigation Was Always a Difficult Art*, and the point at issue there, for me, was the relation between form and matter. Although Hegel was critical of Kantian formalism, Hegelianism is still a formalism. It's a formalism at the level of Spirit, where the idea of *Aufhebung*, or sublation, is the idea of taking on materiality in the form of Spirit, where there's no excess, and no remainder. Blanchot, in *Literature and the Right to Death* – and this essay, which is very important to both of us – talks about two slopes to literature. The first slope is the attempt to incorporate materiality into form, and he identifies that with Hegel and the Marquis de Sade. The second slope is the attempt to let matter be matter – to let matter matter – which still requires a certain form, but a form that allows matter to, as it were, escape. I think we're both committed to that philosophical and literary tradition, with figures like Bataille, Ponge and Wallace Stevens; and, of course, us.

CC: *You often come back to the question of materiality in relation to literature and poetry, both in Simon's work on poetry, particularly* Things Merely Are, *and the various joint declarations where you speak about 'taking the side of things'.*

TMcC: If you look at Ponge's poem on the orange, he asks how we express the orange, in the double sense of the word, meaning represent but also crush, or squeeze. He says that when you do this the orange explodes. First, you get sticky amber liquid over your hand. Secondly, it reprises the shape. Thirdly, it's disappointing, like a premature ejaculation of seed. Fourthly, the husk of the orange is left behind. I think what we both love about Ponge is this sense that even as he's engaging at an almost molecular level with these objects, he's managing a kind of failure in front of them, where the objects always win. And the text becomes, not a record, but a re-enactment of that.

SC: Ponge wants to let the orange, orange.

TMcC: And the sponge, sponge, and so on.

CC: *In the last chapter of* Things Merely Are, *you make the connection between Wallace Stevens's poetry and Terrence Malick's film* The Thin Red Line, *through the notion of calm. I recently watched* The Thin Red Line *again and I was surprised by how unfunny that film is. And what is more, Witt's death seems to be this death where the self coincides with the moment of his death. This seems rather contradictory to me.*

SC: Oh yeah, there's nothing funny in Malick. There's not one joke anywhere.

TMcC: When Sergeant Keck blows his ass off, and his legs come out, that's quite funny.

SC: Yes, in the manner of dramatic irony, maybe. To answer your question: I'm beginning to hate Terrence Malick's films. I think *The New World* from 2005 is rubbish. In retrospect, I fear that I invested far too much in Malick. I think *The Thin Red Line* is disappointing. The war sequences are extraordinary, but other than that I think it's a sort of sentimental, Emersonian, humourless American nature worship, which is part of an ideology of authenticity that I want to reject. It's far too Heideggerian.

TMcC: That's my problem – they just speak philosophy.

SC: Having said that, I devoutly hope that everything I do and say doesn't add up. There's not simply one theoretical line of argument in my work. I've seen philosophers do that, and it can be horrible. So there are contradictions in what I do, different competing threads, obsessions. I'm pulled by temptations, seductions and – increasingly in recent years – by collaborations. We – Tom and I – started to collaborate, not in order that I could say the same shit in different ways; but to try and say something else. Collaborations are really interesting because you find that you're able to say things that you wouldn't otherwise say. In the texts that we've written I can't really decide what's me and what's him – and that's really interesting. The unit of academic literary and intellectual production is the individual. Collaboration is still not really taken seriously because of the logic of branding: *the* artist or *the* thinker, like Brillo or Colgate toothpaste or whatever.

CC: *Let's talk more about this collaboration. How did you end up working together?*

TMcC: We met because I had read Simon's book *Very Little . . . Almost Nothing*, which I thought was very good – kind of brilliant. It's a sensitive and articulate reading of some of the people that most interest me, like Beckett, Blanchot, Derrida and Levinas. For a long time I had been interested in the historical avant-garde – the futurists, the surrealists, all the way up to the situationists. And I've been interested in that kind of collective model of organizing cultural agency where, instead of the bourgeois individual or the great genius artist, you have a committee. What I particularly like with a group like the futurists is that it's not some kind of hippie socialist collective. I mean it's really reactionary – and I just love that. It's really hierarchical and offensive. What's really interesting is that these structures emerge at the same time as the Soviet revolution, and they almost anticipate or shadow the rise of fascism.

SC: Zurich was the home of Dada and the home of Lenin – Lenin-Dada.

TMcC: And these groups also anticipate corporate structures that would arrive later, in the late twentieth century. So what's really interesting is this multiple mirroring of aesthetics, politics and so on. And I just love the art manifesto. As a type of literary form it's brilliant: it's got humour, bombast, arrogance. Marinetti's futurist manifesto is maybe the most brilliant short text I ever read. They crash a car, and they say things like 'death to the future', 'death to the past', 'time and space died yesterday' and all this stuff.

SC: 'Accelerate speed . . .'

TMcC: That's right. It's brilliant stuff. I was interested in this model and so I wrote this manifesto that was almost a pastiche of Marinetti. But because I've been thinking a lot about Blanchot and Derrida, for whom death is a really central theme, I went through the motions of fetishizing death, and not technology, as Marinetti does. I was sort of in the art world at this time, exactly 10 years ago, 1999, and I had been invited to an art fair, where artists were given different tables, to present their work. So I had half of one table and I just handed out these manifestos. And then art galleries, quite soon after that, said, 'great, this is conceptual art, would you like an exhibition?' Another thing is this bureaucratic aesthetic that you find in literature, like in Kafka, or in Conrad or Burroughs or in Pynchon. So when this gallery asked if we wanted an exhibition, since we didn't have any things, I thought we could use the art space as a way to enact these structures. I brought in a committee and a sub-committee, and we began calling in all sorts of cultural practitioners to interrogate them – really quite aggressively – and then making declarations on their art. And Simon was one of the first people I wanted to haul up in front of the committee, because of that book *Very Little . . . Almost Nothing*. About six months later, when we got the first round of purges from the committee, we kicked out our Chief Philosopher, and invited Simon instead.

CC: *Who was your previous Chief Philosopher?*

TMcC: Shane Brighton, who remained a friend.

CC: *So you didn't kill him, which would maybe be more of an INS thing to do?*

TMcC: No, but one of the people we kicked out was an original Experimental Volunteer and we kicked him out for not being dead; and then he tragically got cancer and he recently died. When he knew he was dying, the first thing he did was to demand his post back. But we told him he couldn't have it until he was actually dead, which he now is, and so we're trying to work out a solution.

SC: That's some dramatic irony.

TMcC: So that's how we met.

CC: *You've been writing a couple of pieces together outside INS – one on Shakespeare and one on Joyce. How did those texts come about?*

SC: I did this seminar in Paris, in 2000, which was to do with the introduction of the euro, on money, with Derrida. A couple of people were invited to talk with him about economics. I talked about this distinction that you find in his work that goes back to Aristotle, between economics and chrematistics – between, on the one hand, the law of the home, the household and the domestic realm, the *oikos*; and, on the other, the law of money-making, the art of money-making, *techne chrematistike*, which is what Aristotle also thinks is the principle of corruption. I remember talking to Tom about that over a beer one evening. At the same point I had been invited to give a lecture on Joyce, at the Joyce Symposium in Trieste, and then we decided to do it together, on money: Joyce and money. We began to read *Finnegans Wake* in terms of the logic of chrematistics, thinking about money in relationship to coinage, financial coinage and other forms of coinage. Some people liked it, and some really hated it. It palpably divided the audience. And then we did a second text, which was for an event on Shakespeare and philosophy in Budapest, and that text was also linked to money and coinage in *The Merchant of Venice* and what we call the 'moneying' of love in Shakespeare's sonnets. What is happening in Shakespeare is the transformation of courtly love into commerce, into a whole language of expenditure and loans. Sonnet 4 begins, 'Unthrifty loveliness, why dost thou spend / Upon thyself thy beauty's legacy? / Nature's bequest gives nothing, but doth lend.'

TMcC: The great thing with being able to work in that kind of mode is that it's somewhere between fiction and discourse. The INS is already a fiction, but that doesn't mean it's fake. We delivered this Joint Declaration in New York and I think it went down really well. And then there was a really intelligent article about it, by a guy called Peter Schwenger, who said that while he loved what we were saying, he didn't think it was *us* saying it. He was wrong – it *was* us – but it was a very good idea. So when Tate Britain asked us to do the same thing in London, we thought we could put that into practice; so, we hired actors to be us. And of course they did it much better than we would have done.

CC: *I watched the clip from that event and I must say that the actors were really good.*

SC: Very good.

TMcC: They were also more real. We gave them the answers in advance, to whatever the questions would be, and the remarkable thing was that the first two questions perfectly matched the answers they were given. And the first one was amazing. Every time Derrida stood up to speak in London, over a span of 30 years, there would be some enraged positivist, denouncing him. We had that guy – again: 'You can't prove anything you say, do you think you're clever just because you're using French words?' And he thought he was being authentic. We knew we were being inauthentic; those actors knew they were inauthentic; but he was absolutely inauthentic – re-enacting, reiterating what had been said a million times before.

CC: *It was only really the last question, when someone asked what had happened to Simon's hair and your tie, which made any sense.*

TMcC: Yeah, but they knew us.

CC: *What was the response following from this event?*

SC: Some people got angry.

TMcC: A couple of people were angry. People in the art world got it. In London now, the art world is the intelligent place, where literature is being read and discussed. *Remainder* was first published by an art press, and not by a mainstream press.

CC: *They said it was too literary.*

TMcC: That's right.

SC: The art world was your necronautical vehicle, Tom.

TMcC: Absolutely. I mean that's the place. The art world is the umbrella arena where you can bring other things in and they become meaningful. So the art people got our Declaration. They understand playfulness, misdirection – and that's the stuff that really mattered. There were some people from the *Times Literary Supplement* there and one of them was furious. She came up afterwards and said we were being dis-honest and that we were mocking the audience. Simon was simultaneously giving an interview in New York, just at that moment, only to press the point that it could not have been him. I was at the Tate in London. But it was odd, because it would have been so much easier for us to do it ourselves. It was very complex: we had to train the actors, we had to persuade the Tate and there were a lot of logistics to be managed. And also, I didn't see it as mocking at all. There were elements of humour, definitely, but it was a sincere and kind of authentic enactment of what we were saying. We were making it happen, rather than just talking about it. We were playing it out in a way that we couldn't control; we didn't know what the questions were going to be. So that response was kind of strange. But then, the *Times Literary Supplement* is not what it used to be.

CC: *Did you get any response from the world of philosophy?*

SC: Resounding silence, as is usually the case.

CC: *Do you agree, Simon, that the art world is where things happen?*

SC: For me, that's more and more the case. We're sitting right now in a university, in the business school at Queen Mary, University of London. Universities are business schools. At least business schools say they're business schools, which is more honest than the rest of the rubbish. And these are places where you can no longer think. You're not encouraged to think – it's not what you're supposed to do. You are simply meant to produce. At a certain point, not that long ago, universities were places where thinking took place. Perhaps this seems an absurd and ludicrous proposition. But thinking happened, particularly in experimental universities, that developed in the 1960s, in England: Essex, Sussex, Warwick and the rest, which are now tedious and mediocre business schools. So it has become harder and harder to think in universities. Something has shifted in culture and the art world has become, at least in certain places, a privileged site of cultural articulation, for the meanings attached to culture. But to finish Tom's story, after the Tate Britain Declaration, we then decided that we would franchise the declaration because other institutions might be interested. So, thanks to our Minister of Propaganda, Anthony Auerbach, and Laura Hopkins, our Environmental Engineer, we put together an enactment manual. And about this time we had been asked by the Athens Biennale to do a version with Greek actors. I went there to make sure it was all done correctly, which it was, with extraordinary accuracy and precision. The next thing will probably be the *Berlin Aerial Surveillance Project* connected with some events in theatres in Berlin, though we're opposed to theatres. We're anti-theatre.

TMcC: We're interested only in car-parks. Really, car-parks are very interesting places, full of technology.

CC: *Car-parks? This brings us to another theme that seems to be of great interest to you, namely technology and how technology brings new forms of being. Today, there's the hope – and fear – that technology can alter the human being, so that eventually it will morph into a post-human.*

TMcC: I'm totally against that, not because technology can make us un-human. Desire is not mediated by technology; it's enacted through technology. Desire is already a technology. *Techne*, in Heidegger, means revealing – that's what the Greek term means: bringing it out into the world. What's interesting is the enmeshing of the self and technology; that's what I love in Pynchon, in *Gravity's Rainbow*, where scientists are even fucking their instruments. Technology is automatically a critique of humanism because it shows that we are not self-efficient, but, rather, networked.

SC: In a sense INS is anti-humanist, but it is also anti post-humanism.

TMcC: Exactly, because post-humanism is just an extension of humanism; it's humanism 2.0.

SC: Post-humanism is a dreadful fantasy, which you find reproduced in corporations, like universities. I mean, the response to the question of post-humanism is the same as my response to the question of happiness: very nice, but not for us. We are eminently human, and this is nothing to be proud of. To be human is to be that experience of repetition and non-self-coincidence that constitutes us. The fantasy of becoming God, the fantasy of becoming nothing or the fantasy of becoming post-human: they are all the same. And people who waste their time on such fantasies should be pitied and then ignored. You get the same fantasy in neuroscience, and in New Age, and in other things like that. I think these are all pernicious things, which need to be nailed. Fantasies about the future – who cares?

TMcC: That's what J. G. Ballard said, that the future is boring.

SC: The future is pernicious because the function of ideology is always to suture over gaps and divisions, and to give us a feeling of unity and purpose, which is always directed towards the future. In particular the ideology of capitalism, but also anti-capitalism: they are both directed towards an ideology of the future. I think what we have to do is to refuse the idea of the future. What we should be concerned with is the cultivation of the past, of memory. The future is about amnesia, and that's what's behind this ludicrous love affair with technology and forms of social networking and all that nonsense – these are forms of oblivion, the desire for oblivion. The future is the enemy of radical thought. It prevents interesting thinking. It's reactionary.

CC: *How about the opposite reaction to technology, which you find in the writings of Jacques Ellul and Heidegger, where modern technology is seen as ruining the condition of possibility for authenticity?*

SC: That's another thing I want to refuse. You certainly find that in Ellul – and in Heidegger as well. I mean, in Heidegger, you get this idea that 'where the danger is, the saving power also grows'. The contrast between danger and saving power is a false opposition. Technology is not a danger and there is no saving power in opposition to it. There is no essence to technology that we can grasp in order to release humanity from its grip. It becomes a question of thinking the intrication between the human and the technological. And I think another fantasy is the fantasy of the biological. You can say any sort of stupid weird shit on the radio about biology or neuroscience, and people will just lap it up. It's a shocking situation because people want to believe that there is some other place, not necessarily God, but some deterministic narrative where we end up with some picture of the brain or some picture of the living organism where finally everything will be in place and then we will be able to do this, this and this – it's nonsense.

TMcC: It's idiocy. Neuroscience is one of the biggest follies of our era, or the idea that you can transfer neuroscience to the cultural arena. It's a category mistake. We don't think in our brains, we think in language and culture. If you want to understand meaning in the world, and the history of meaning, you've got to read *Antigone* and then you've got to read Hegel and then you've got to read Lacan. You can't slice up anyone's brain, not even Sophocles', and then understand meaning. If you take a bit of Joyce's brain and put it under a microscope, it's not going to explain *Finnegans Wake*. It's absolute idiocy, but an idiocy that has a lot of currency simply because people don't want to think. They want easy answers. It's a form of a God; it's a form of absolute certainty that will kind of flatten all the complexity of culture, and the beauty of it as well.

CC: *And neuroscience seems to have a very close relation to the future and progress?*

SC: The angel of history faces the future, backwards; and the storm that's blowing through its wings is that dreadful thing called progress, as Benjamin says. I don't think it's easy, but we should as rigorously as possible divest ourselves of this ideology of the future and the cult of progress. Progress is an idea, which is only a couple of hundred years old, and it's a very bad idea. The sooner we're rid of it the better. But this is the way things are structured ideologically. The way to get attention is to announce that, within 20 years, human beings will live until they are 120 years old.

TMcC: We need to replace progress with repetition. That would be a much healthier world. Think of the Renaissance. Renaissance means rebirth. What they did was to say: 'Look at these Greeks. It's great! Look at all this stuff that has been stuffed in under barrels for 2,000 years. Fucking brilliant! Let's do it!' And Shakespeare's plays: there's no claim to something new; he's rewriting Ovid or he's taking speeches straight out of the Roman parliament. You even get this scene, from *A Midsummer Night's Dream*, with a bunch of Greeks sitting around watching Greek theatre: that's what nowadays would be called postmodern; it's super-aware of its own embedding within media.

SC: And Greek tragedy, which for both of us is very impor-tant, is about repetition. And about technology. *The Oresteia* begins with the technological transmission of a message through a series of beacons, like a radio signal.

TMcC: Yes. Half of the first act describes how the message of Greek victory has got from Troy to Argos.

SC: Tragedy is about media and communication and it's about a human situation defined by memory and repetition.

TMcC: Actually, having said how crap theatre is, I was dragged along to see a production of *Agamemnon* a few years ago, and it was very good. The director had a very clever idea of having the chorus played as journalists. That's what the chorus is: it's a kind of media archive that curates memory; and again, this is what's important: fuck the future, it's about curating and bringing back, it's about reactivating memory.

CC: *So it's in this respect that you find technology interesting, as a way to curate the past?*

TMcC: Exactly!

CC: *To come back to the question of authenticity: there's an interesting relationship between the catastrophe and authenticity. Is there an authenticity of the catastrophe?*

TMcC: That's an interesting question. When I was researching *Remainder* and was reading stuff about trauma, not necessarily philosophy, but psychology and about actual accounts of post-traumatic stress disorder – and I talked to people who had been in accidents – there was one thing that kept coming up, and that was the idea that only the catastrophe seems real afterward. It's a very common syndrome among people who come home from a war zone, or who have been in a car or plane crash. Suddenly life doesn't seem real. Warhol famously said, 'Ever since being shot I've felt like I'm just watching television.' The experience is that none of this is real, it's all just fake; only *that* was real. It doesn't mean that it *is* real, but that it stands in the place of the real. Memory is always a narrative, we have this mechanism in our brains that turns ones and zeros into a narrative thread, which is memory. Interestingly, very often in cases of trauma, that part goes off to strike. So you got the data, but it has not been dealt with. And the catastrophic event keeps coming back. That gap, or absence, that few seconds of silence on the tape, become real; since everything else that is on the tape is fake, that gap must be real. This is a construct, a completely artificial construction. But it's interesting that the event then stands in the place of authenticity.

SC: The question is whether the catastrophe is the exception or the rule, whether the catastrophe is something which induces the sense of unreality in reality. This is what Freud identifies as the compulsion to repeat, so there's a direct connection between the trauma and repetition. We're both very concerned with this thematic of repetition in our work. In the case of *Remainder* the hero remembers very little . . . almost nothing of the accident. And he's trying to re-enact what it means to be human. I see *Remainder* as this long hymn to inauthenticity. Everything is second hand. The world is full of usurpers and frauds. And then there's the famous moment in the bathroom, where he looks at the crack and then the world begins to configure itself – which might be real, it might not be real. It's not clear. And the interesting question is whether the condition of the protagonist in *Remainder* is a general condition of human beings or an exception. Which then raises the issue that defines the hero in *Remainder* of the longing for the essential authenticity of existence, a longing for an experience of fluency, where actions and objects are merged, and where nothing is separated from me. The experience that the protagonist in *Remainder* is after is this feeling of tingling – no distance separating me from reality, no self-reflection, no detours. It's a fantasy of authenticity. The question is whether that's the exception or the rule.

TMcC: I think it's the rule. The hero in *Remainder* has that conversation with his friend, when he watches all the other people coming out of the airport striking a pose, or being cool in Soho; it's like everyone is re-enacting moments from ads or movies they've seen. And he realizes he's just the same as everyone else. He's just *more* normal. He's exceptional in the intensity of his normalness. In a way, I think he's kind of heroic, in a very inauthentic way, because he pushes the logic of our inauthentic world of late capitalism, he pushes it absolutely to its limit. He's so loyal to the loyalty cards that he ends up killing everyone.

CC: *It seems as if pushing things to the extreme, as the hero in* Remainder *clearly does, is also a way to assume full responsibility, almost a sort of infinite responsibility that you would find in Levinas.*

TMcC: True. It was through Simon's work that I got into Levinas. I read Simon's *Levinas' Basic Philosophical Writings,* and it's brilliant stuff. Levinas has a vision of ethics, which is completely tied in with trauma, and completely tied in with repetition, and it's not about a self-sufficient subject being moral. It's about subjectivity being endlessly ruptured and interrupted by the demand of the other, to which you have to respond. And I think the hero in *Remainder* – it's almost perverse to say this, because in one sense he's a fascist, he kills people and so on – is an ethical subject. When he re-enacts the death of this drug-dealer, whom the police had done the minimum of work with – they photographed the scene, wiped the blood away and opened up the street for traffic – he says: 'No, that won't do! Something has happened here and we need to go back to it again, again and again. Endlessly.' That's the only adequate response, not to explain it, but opening up that space. It was not until after I had written the book that I read Levinas. But I thought, 'Yeah, that's what I meant.'

SC: It's a sense of recurrence. The self as recurrence, or as repetition, which is still the way I try and think about this in relationship to the experience of conscience; not as a good conscience, but conscience as an open wound, which you can't stop picking at – picking at the scabs, making it bleed. It's something that, in a sense, we are powerless over; we're compelled to repeat in that way. And that's what's difficult in literature and other things that we like and use. What we're being taken back to is this state of repetition, trauma and catastrophe that in a way forces human beings to confront themselves and their powerlessness and their responsibility. If morality becomes a question, as it is on BBC Radio 4, of nicely educated people with shrill voices making choices between different courses of action and being able to account for them, then this is awful. I think the subject is a subject that can't decide and has to decide; it's compelled to be responsible, but flees that responsibility.

Bibliography

Works by Simon Critchley referred to in this book

The Ethics of Deconstruction: Derrida and Levinas (Oxford: Blackwell, 1992); rev. and expanded edn, with three new appendices (Edinburgh: Edinburgh University Press, 1999).

Very Little . . . Almost Nothing: Death, Philosophy, Literature (London and New York: Routledge, 1997; rev. and expanded 2nd edn, 2004).

Ethics–Politics–Subjectivity. Essays on Derrida, Levinas and Contemporary French Thought (London: Verso, 1999; reissued in Verso's Radical Thinkers series, 2009).

Continental Philosophy. A Very Short Introduction (Oxford: Oxford University Press, 2001).

On Humour (London and New York: Routledge, 2002).

Things Merely Are – Philosophy in the Poetry of Wallace Stevens (London and New York: Routledge, 2005).

Infinitely Demanding. Ethics of Commitment, Politics of Resistance (London and New York: Verso, 2007).

The Book of Dead Philosophers (London: Granta, 2008; New York: Vintage Books, 2009).

On Heidegger's Being and Time, with Reiner Schürmann, ed. Stephen Levine (London and New York: Routledge, 2008).

The Faith of the Faithless (Cambridge MA: Harvard University Press, 2011).

'I Want to Die, I Hate my Life – Phaedra's Malaise', *New Literary History*, 35/1 (Winter 2004): 17–40.

'Of Chrematology – on Joyce and Money', with Tom McCarthy, *Hypermedia Joyce Studies*, 4/1 (July 2003).

'To Be or Not To Be Is Not the Question', *Film-Philosophy*, 11/2 (2007): 108–21.

'Universal Shylockery – Money and Morality in *The Merchant of Venice*', with Tom McCarthy, *Diacritics*, 34/1 (Spring 2004 [appeared 2006]): 3–17.

'Noises Off – On Ibsen', *Ibsen Studies*, 7/2 (2007): 132–49.

'Tate Declaration on Inauthenticity', International Necronautical Society, with Tom McCarthy, in Nicolas Bourriaud, ed., *Altermodern* (London: Tate Publishing, 2009), pp. 170–84.

'Mystical Anarchism', *Critical Horizons*, 10/2 (2009): 272–306.

'The Catechism of the Citizen: Politics, Law and Religion In, After, With and Against Rousseau', *Law and Humanities*, 1/1 (Summer 2007): 79–109.

'What is the Hole Inside the Hole? On David Lynch's *Inland Empire*', with Jamieson Webster, *Bedeutung*, 3; available at: www.bedeutung.co.uk/index.php?option=com_ content&view=article&id=43:what-is-the-hole-inside-the-hole&catid=8:issue-3-contents&Itemid=20.

'Barack Obama and the American Void', *Harper's Magazine*, 1902 (November 2008): 17–20.

Works by Tom McCarthy

Navigation Was Always a Difficult Art (London: Vargas Organization, 2002).

Calling All Agents (London: Vargas Organization, 2003).

Remainder (Paris: Metronome Press, 2005; London: Alma Books, 2006; New York: Vintage, 2007).

Tintin and the Secret of Literature (London: Granta, 2006; Berkeley: Counterpoint, 2008).

Men in Space (London: Alma Books, 2007).

C (London: Jonathan Cape, 2010; New York: Knopf, 2010).

Referenced works

Arendt, Hannah (1987). *The Life of the Mind*, 2 vols. (New York: Harcourt Brace Jovanovich).

Aristotle (1985). *Nicomachean Ethics*, trans, Terence Irwin (Indianapolis: Hackett Publishing Company).

Augustine (1960). *The Confessions of St Augustine*, trans. J. K. Ryan (New York: Doubleday).

Bakhtin, Mikhail (1968). *Rabelais and His World* (Cambridge, MA: MIT Press).

Beckett, Samuel (1970). *Watt* (London: Calder).

Beckett, Samuel (1979). *Molloy, Malone Dies, The Unnameable* (London: Picador).

Beckett, Samuel (1986). *The Complete Dramatic Works* (London: Faber).

Bergson, Henri (1980). *Laughter* (Baltimore: Johns Hopkins University Press).

Blanchot, Maurice (1949). *La Part du feu.* (Paris: Gallimard).

Blanchot, Maurice (1981). 'Literature and the Right to Death', in *The Gaze of Orpheus and Other Literary Essays*, trans. Lydia Davis (Barrytown, NY: Station Hill Press).

Blanchot, Maurice (1994). *L'Instant de ma mort* (Montpellier: Fata Morgana).

Boethius (1969). *The Consolation of Philosophy*, trans. V. E. Watts (London: Penguin).

Breton, André (1966). *Anthologie de l'humour noir* (Paris: Jean-Jacques Pauvert).

Carson, Anne (2002). 'Decreation: How Women Like Sappho, Marguerite Porete and Simone Weil Tell God', *Common Knowledge,* Vol. 8 No. 1 pp. 188–201.

Cohn, Norman (1970). *The Pursuit of the Millennium: Revolutionary Millenarians and Mystical Anarchists of the Middle Ages*, rev. and expanded edn (London: Temple Smith).

Comité invisible (2007). *L'Insurrection qui vient* (Paris: La Fabrique Editions). Available in English as *The Coming Insurrection*, http://tarnac9.wordpress.com/texts/the-coming-insurrection/ (accessed June 2009).

Conrad, Joseph (1924). *Nostromo* (New York: Doubleday, Page).

Derrida, Jacques (1978). 'Violence and Metaphysics', in *Writing and Difference*, trans. A. Bass (Chicago: University of Chicago Press).

Derrida, Jacques (1986). *Mémoires for Paul de Man*, trans. C. Lindsay, J. Culler and E. Cadava (New York: Columbia University Press).

Diogenes, L. (2005–6). *The Lives of Eminent Philosophers*, trans. R. D. Hicks, 2 vols (Cambridge, MA: Harvard University Press).

Eliot, T. S. (1990). *The Waste Land: A Facsimile and Transcript of the Original Drafts Including the Annotations of Ezra Pound*, ed. Valerie Eliot (London: Faber & Faber).

Eliot, T. S. (1991). *Collected Poems 1909–1962* (New York: Harcourt Brace).

Foucault, Michel (1978). *The History of Sexuality*, Vol. 1: *An Introduction*, trans R. Hurley (New York: Pantheon).

Freud, Sigmund (1953–1974). 'Mourning and Melancholia', in *The Standard Edition of the Complete Psychological Works of Sigmund Freud, XIV*, ed. J. Strachey (London: Hogarth Press).

Freud, Sigmund (1953–1974). 'On Narcissism', in *The Standard Edition of the Complete Psychological Works of Sigmund Freud, XIV*, ed. J. Strachey (London: Hogarth Press).

Freud, Sigmund (1953–1974). 'On the Tendency To Debasement in the Sphere of Love' in *The Standard Edition of the Complete Psychological Works of Sigmund Freud, XIV*, ed. J. Strachey (London: Hogarth Press).

Freud, Sigmund (1976). *Jokes and Their Relation to the Unconscious* (London: Penguin).

Freud, Sigmund (1985). 'Humour', in *Art and Literature* (London: Penguin).

Freud, Sigmund (1992). *Der Witz und seine Beziehung zum Unbewußten. Der Humor* (Frankfurt: Fischer).

Gray, John (2003). *Straw Dogs: Thoughts on Humans and Other Animals* (London: Granta).

Gray, John (2007). *Black Mass: Apocalyptic Religion and the Death of Utopia* (New York: Farrar, Straus & Giroux).

Griffiths, Trevor (1976). *Comedians* (Faber: London).

Hegel, G. W. F. (1977). *Phenomenology of Spirit*, trans. A. V. Miller (Oxford: Oxford University Press: Oxford).

Heidegger Martin (1959). *The Introduction to Metaphysics*, trans. R. Manheim (New Haven: Yale University Press).

Heidegger, Martin (1980). *Being and Time*, trans. J. Macquarrie and E. Robinson. (Blackwell: Oxford).

Hobbes, Thomas (1991). *Leviathan*, ed. R. Tuck (Cambridge: Cambridge University Press).

Husserl, E. (1954). *The Crisis of the European Sciences* (Evanston: Northwestern University Press).

Joyce, James (1986). *Ulysses*, ed. H. Walter Gabler (New York: Random).

Kafka, Franz (1971). *The Trial* (New York: Schocken Books).

Kant, Immanuel (1929). *Critique of Pure Reason* (London: Macmillan).

Kant, Immanuel (1952) *The Critique of Judgment*, trans. J. C. Meredith (Oxford: Oxford University Press).

Kant, Immanuel (1993). *Critique of Practical Reason* (New York: Macmillan).

Kundera, Milan (2001). *The Book of Laughter and Forgetting* (London: Penguin).

Lacan, Jacques (1975[1962–3]). *The Seminar, Book XX: Encore* (Paris: Seuil).

Lacan, Jacques (1992[1959–60]). *The Seminar, Book VII: The Ethics of Psychoanalysis* (London: Routledge).

Landauer G. (2007). 'Anarchic Thoughts on Anarchism',

trans. J. Cohn and G. Kuhn, *Perspectives on Anarchist Theory*, 6: 84–91. First published as 'Anarchische Gedanken über Anarchismus' in *Zukunft* (26 October 1901): 134–40.

Levinas, E. (1987). *Collected Philosophical Papers*, trans. Alphonso Lingis (Dordrecht: Kluwer).

Lucretius (1994). *On the Nature of the Universe*, trans. R. E. Latham (London: Penguin).

Maurice Blanchot (1955). *L'Espace littéraire* (Paris: Gallimard).

Montaigne, M. (1976). *The Complete Essays of Montaigne*, trans. Donald M. Frame (Stanford: Stanford University Press).

Nietzsche, F. (1967). *On the Genealogy of Morals*, trans. Walter Kaufmann (New York: Vintage).

Pessoa, Fernando (2002). *The Book of Disquiet*, trans. R. Zenith (London: Penguin Classics).

Plato (1914). *Euthyphro, Apology, Crito, Phaedo, Phaedrus*, trans. Harold North Fowler. (Cambridge, MA: Harvard University Press).

Plessner, H. (1982). 'Das Lächeln', in *Mit anderen Augen. Aspekte einer philosophischen Anthropologie* (Stuttgart: Reclam).

Plessner, Helmuth (1982). *Lachen und Weinen, Gesammelte Schriften*, vol. 7 (Frankfurt: Suhrkamp).

Ponge, Francis (1948). *Le Parti pris des choses, suivi de poèmes* (Paris: Gallimard).

Pope, Alexander (1972). 'The Rape of the Lock', in Geoffrey Tillotson, ed., *Poems of Alexander Pope* (New Haven: Yale University Press).

Porete, Marguerite (1993). *The Mirror of Simple Souls*, trans. E. Babinsky (Mahwah, NJ: Paulist Press).

Pynchon, Thomas (1973). *Gravity's Rainbow* (London: Picador).

Racine, Jean (1963). *Phaedra and Other Plays*, trans. J. Cairncross (London: Penguin).

Rousseau, Jean-Jacques (1997). *The Discourses and Other Early Political Writings*, ed. V. Gourevitch (Cambridge: Cambridge University Press).

Schelling, Friedrich Wilhelm Joseph von (1980). 'Philosophical Letters on Dogmatism and Criticism', in *The Unconditional in Human Knowledge: Four Early Essays: 1994–1996*, trans. Fritz Marti. (Lewisburg: Bucknell University Press).

Schmitt, Carl (2006). *Political Theology: Four Chapters on the Concept of Sovereignty*, trans. G. Schwab. (Chicago: University of Chicago Press)

Shakespeare, William (1955). *The Merchant of Venice*, ed. J. R. Brown (London: Methuen).

Shakespeare, William (1994). *A Midsummer Night's Dream*, ed. P. Holland (Oxford: Oxford University Press).

Spinoza, Benedict de (1997). *Ethics*, trans. C. D. N. Costa (Penguin: London).

Sterne, Laurence (1955). *The Life and Opinions of Tristram Shandy, Gentleman*, ed. M. and J. New (Penguin: London).

Stevens, Wallace (1967). *The Palm at the End of the Mind* (New York: Vintage).

Stevens, Wallace (1989). *Opus posthumous*, ed. M. J. Bates (New York: Knopf).

Swift, Jonathan (1967). *Gulliver's Travels* (Penguin: London).

Vanegiem, R. (1994). *The Movement of the Free Spirit*, trans. R. Cherry and I. Patterson (New York: Zone Books).

Wilde, Oscar (1962). 'De Profundis' *The Letters of Oscar Wilde*, ed. R. Hart-Davis (New York: Harcourt, Brace and World).

Wittgenstein, Ludwig (1961). *Tractatus Logico-Philosophicus*, trans. D. F. Pears and B. F. McGuiness (London: Routledge).

Index

Index

Index

Rose, Gillian, 22
Rosset, Clement, 15
Rousseau, Jean-Jacques, viii, 23, 31

Sappho, 66
Sartre, Jean-Paul, 11, 52
Schelling, F. W. J., 96
Schlegel, Friedrich, 98
Schmitt, Carl, 99
Scholem, 67
Schopenhauer, Arthur, 86
Schürman, Reiner, 23
Schwenger, Peter, 112
Seneca, 58
Sex Pistols, The, 9
Shakespeare, William, 97, 111, 112, 118
Simmons, John, 77
Sjöholm, Cecilia, 20
Socrates, 1, 27, 53, 55, 57, 60, 72
Sophocles, 96, 97, 117
Spencer, Herbert, 86
Spinoza, Baruch, 1, 37, 50, 54, 104
St Augustine, 45, 56, 57, 60
St Francis, 75

St Paul, 45, 56, 68, 69
Sterne, Laurence, 97
Stevens, Wallace, 21, 107
Swift, Jonathan, 87, 88, 92, 97

Tangerine Dream, 8
Teresa of Avila, 64
Thatcher, Margaret, 13, 15
Tosel, André, 15

Vaneigem, Raoul, 100
Vibrators, The 9
Virgil, 97

Walken, Christopher, 72
Warhol, Andy, 119, 120
Webster, Jamieson, xii
Weil, Simone, 66
Weston, Mike, 14
Wilde, Oscar, 66
Willis, Bruce, 72
Wire, 9
Wittgenstein, Ludwig, 28, 54, 57
Wood, David, 22

Žižek, Slavoj, vii